The Art of Street Riding

ISBN 978-0-578-04830-7

Dedicated to

all those who have passed along to me the tips, tricks and techniques that have made me the rider that I am. It is through their friendship, generosity and sharing spirit that I am able to write this book.

Special Acknowledgements

I wish to thank my editorial volunteers who provided countless pieces of fantastic advice and input throughout the writing process

Dan Carter
Ed Williams
Marc McNaughton

And I also wish to thank all the photographic contributors whose passion and enthusiasm for motorcycling is displayed in the awe-inspiring images that you see presented throughout this book.

Roger Koster
Ty Reed
Robert Douglas Smith
Brad Esler
Chris Hornberger
David Wedel
Global Rider
Wayne Swanson
Tom Grigg
John Alderman
Tom Snyder
Kevin VanHoozier
Eric Millard
Ken Denton
Harry K. Berman III
William Sutton
Jeffery Gilbert
Charles Roberts
James Grant
Don Wilcox
Joseph Volltrauer
Jeff Geske
Aerostich
Brad Williams
Howard Dyke
Colleen First

LEGAL DISCLAIMER

Motorcycles are inherently dangerous machines with the power to injure, maim or kill the rider or others regardless of how safe the rider may try to be. Any accident can be fatal, no matter how minor it may seem. There is no such thing as "safe motorcycling".

This book encourages risk-conscious riding and suggests actions, approaches, methods, and activities, which- while tending to assist riders in becoming safer- will undoubtedly place the rider at risk. All of these suggestions, like every action in motorcycling, may result in injury or death. The methods, concepts and techniques presented are not suitable for all riders nor for any riders at all times.

This book has two goals: (1) to foster discussion of the finer points of street riding and (2) to provide alternative ideas and food for thought to assist riders in developing their own ability to critically assess riding strategies, methods and techniques. As a reader of this book or disseminator of the information contained herein, you hereby agree it is your sole responsibility to assess for yourself and others the reasonableness and advisability of all the information provided herein. The author is not able to assess your or others' experience, knowledge, abilities, or riding conditions. The suggestions contained in this book at times may be specific in nature and tailored to a particular type of rider. Before taking any advice from this book, it is critical that you discuss the topics with other experienced riders and instructors who are known to you and can offer more personalized advice, which takes into consideration the rider's experience level, locale, riding preferences, abilities, and other factors which cannot be adequately covered by this book.

Ultimately, it is solely the reader/rider's decision how, where, and when to ride. The author disclaims all responsibility for any injury, death, accident or incident that results from the information provided by this book. By reading this book, you agree to take sole responsibility for your actions on a motorcycle.

PREFACE

As I saw friends and acquaintances get involved in motorcycling, I felt excited for them but also experienced considerable trepidation: I know that the first few months on the road present many dangerous lessons to be learned. To cope with this dangerous, possibly lethal, time in every rider's career, I continue to strongly urge everyone interested in riding to seek out professional instruction to learn the basics and form a basis for safer riding. However, this is only the beginning.

Experienced riders have techniques and tricks they perform consistently to help them manage the risks of riding. Normally, these methods are learned by riders on their own, developed by personal experience out of necessity. They are understood by each rider on an intuitive level which is seldom, if ever, put into words. As I wrote this book, it developed into a way to take a number of these habits and distill them into something others can learn from; I worked to create these frameworks to accelerate the learning process for other riders facing the risks and challenges of the street.

Information was pulled from a variety of sources: from my experiences in aviation, as an all-weather motorcycle commuter in a major U.S. city, and as a long-distance rider and driver who has frequently traveled hundreds of miles in a day. Being an analytical rider, every ride I took became a study in risk management, seeking to bring home new ideas and concepts in street riding. Much of the information will not be new to experienced riders and it might be tempting to read through this book and say to yourself, "I already know that concept." But the details matter. It is news to no one that streets are a dangerous place to ride, but there is nuance in the way that we, as motorcyclists, can interact with cars and cope with the varied risks.

If you've been riding for a few years, you are at least peripherally aware of all the concepts in this book. What is new, however, is the way you can look at these concepts. I invite you to take these concepts to the next level and try them out. View the hazards discussed with greater suspicion and respect than you did before. Try some of these concepts on, just as you would try on a new jacket, and see how they fit. Do they make you a better rider? When you pay more attention to certain hazards, or when you make decisions based on the risk factors presented in this book, do you feel safer? Do you feel more in control of the situations you face?

This book takes only a hodge-podge approach to risk assessment. It focuses on some of the larger and more advanced hazards and issues that riders face, but is not an all-inclusive text on motorcycling and it is certainly not a substitute for classes and the lessons laid out by large committees of highly experienced riders. What is presented here is merely a continuation of what should be an ongoing process for all riders– developing one's own ideas and concepts of risk-conscious riding.

Every time you get on a motorcycle, you must accept the risk and only consider all the advice you've received in light of your present situation. You must also continue to seek out information from other sources, always diligently assessing the risk for yourself as you grow as a rider. Do not make decisions based upon what I propose in this book. Make the decisions instead based upon your wisdom and riding experience. Accept, for now, only those parts of this book that ring true to you and help you to immediately become a safer rider. The rest, should be discussed with others, integrating their advice and insight with all the other information you have received from other sources.

This book is my attempt to provide some ideas for consideration. I write this book not as a self-proclaimed expert, but as someone who has distilled some degree of experience into a more easily digestible series of paragraphs, bullet points, diagrams, pictures, and sidebars. Take it as opinion, not as fact. If you do this, the ideas presented within this book will undoubtedly help you learn what works for you and what is safer for you. It will foster accelerated appreciation for the risks we all face on the streets.

Always ride safe.

CONTENTS

INTRODUCTION

There is shockingly little logic that can be used to justify the decision to ride a motorcycle, especially on the street. It is something that must be understood on a deep instinctive level and for many riders it is something we are born with or something that develops very early on. For most, the dangers of motorcycling are inextricably intertwined with the experience; if you take away the danger, you take away much of the pleasure. However, even though the danger may be part of the attraction, risk management is still necessary. If riders intend to continue riding year after year, they must learn the techniques, tips, and tricks that will keep them safe to continue enjoying the experience. Riding schools and text books are an excellent start, and this book may be the next step forward.

In other high risk activities such as flying, it is commonly acknowledged that participants go through four phases of experience. The four phases are described as follows:

Inexperience
Competence
Over-Confidence
Confidence

The process of learning to ride begins with an exceptionally hazardous phase where participants lack the developed skill and experience necessary to consistently avoid danger. During this Inexperienced phase, the rider's inexperience is only counter-balanced by their cautiousness.

After some period of time, riders begin to gain mastery over the basic skills and the frequency of accidents and injury declines and riders begin to enter the stage of Competence. At this stage, riders are more comfortable on the seat and are able to process more information and analyze situations with greater ease.

However, as more time passes, the participants become complacent toward the dangers and over-confident in their skills. This commonly leads to another period of heightened risk which can be described as the Over-Confident phase. During this phase, riders tend to push themselves and their motorcycle a little bit harder, trying to find the limits of their riding ability. In some ways, this phase is more dangerous than the first phase because over-confident riders tend to travel at higher speeds and ride more aggressively than new riders. Therefore, accidents experienced by riders during this phase tend to be worse than the accidents encountered when first starting out.

Eventually, riders begin to find their personal limits and those of the bike. The extreme challenge of mastering a bike gives way to the pleasures of riding and the number of accidents a motorcyclist is likely to face will begin to slowly and steadily decline.

This book is written for experienced riders in the latter three categories who have already availed themselves of the courses that are out there for beginning riders and have passed the stage of inexperience. At these next three stages, riders should be able to assess safety factors and risk for themselves. Therefore it is not necessary to provide a framework for all the possible risks that exist on the street. Instead, this book considers a number of the biggest risks and delves deeper into some ways that the dangers can be mitigated through risk-conscious riding. This book will assist riders in coming to a deeper understanding of the factors present in particularly hazardous situations and develop frameworks for analyzing many of these risks consciously.

This book provides four key frameworks for riders. The first framework is for the different types of risks faced by riders (Chapter 1). The purpose of this first framework is to create a functional map of the landscape of risk, describing what it looks like at different times, where it comes from, and how riders should plan for it in advance. By viewing risk as an ongoing aspect of riding, rather than something that pops up from time to time, riders can become more attuned to the risks that exist on the street.

The second framework is for street hazards (Chapters 2 and 3). This framework begins with the consideration of seven common and easily-identifiable hazards which pose clear identifiable risks to the motorcyclist. The section then considers the greatest of all street hazards- the intersection- and discusses a number of unique and dangerous situations that all come together to form the perfect storm of dangerous situations.

The third framework is for riding skills (Chapters 4 and 5) and it considers the skills that are commonly used by all motorcyclists and begins to discuss and review some bike control skills as well as providing some unique views on how riders can achieve greater control over their riding abilities.

The fourth framework is human factors (Chapters 6 through 9). Without a doubt, the human factors aspect of riding is the most critical. With the reliability of modern motorcycles and the capabilities of their systems, the rider is clearly the weakest link. The human body's weaknesses are well known, and is extremely important to learn to recognize these weaknesses consistently before they can ever create a substantial danger for the rider. In addition to physical limitations, psychological limitations can be equally, or even more, debilitating for a rider. Taking these considerations into account and learning how to practice identifying them allow riders to dramatically increase their safety by assessing why they ride the way they do and also why they might sometimes want to think twice before getting on a motorcycle.

Within each of these frameworks is a wealth of tips, tricks, and considerations that are not available from other sources. There is also a considerable amount of good, solid advice derived from practical riding experience. With the new frameworks for riding, you will develop greater risk-assessment skills that can potentially save a life and increase your confidence every time you throw a leg over a motorcycle.

THREE TYPES OF RISK 1

Fog on a two lane road. What kinds of risks might you encounter? What might other animals or other vehicles do as a result of the fog which may place you at greater risk? How can you prepare in advance for these types of risk?

Think back to a time when you were taken by surprise while riding, when some hazard seemed to come out of nowhere. As the surprise began to unfold before your eyes, you did what riders do regularly on the street– you attempted to make adjustments to avoid the hazard. However, just before that moment began, there were undoubtedly subtle indications that certain unusual events were more likely than others. And if you had been tuned-in to these subtle hints surrounding you, it would have been possible to begin planning for the hazard before it even came into sight.

The sooner a hazard is identified, the more time the rider will have to react. One valuable method of improving hazard identification is based on the classification of different types of risk. For this book, external risks are broken down into three distinct stages, each with different strategies for mitigation. The first stage is Environmental Risk. This is the general unspecific risk that is omnipresent for motorcyclists: the unknown and often random dangers that lurk somewhere up the road. The second stage is situational risk. Situational risk is the identified hazard, far up the road, to which the rider devotes additional attention and care in anticipation of a potentially hazardous situation. The third stage is tactical risk. Tactical risk is the split-second emergency that demands immediate and precise reaction.

n wide open country, what kinds of angers might you expect to encounter? Iow will you prepare yourself for these ossibilities? Do you consistently tweak our pace on a minute-by-minute basis to ccount for changing levels of risk?

The three stages of risk describe the same dangers, but at different times and places, reflecting different levels of awareness and urgency. By using this structure to carefully evaluate external risks, riders can make better decisions about the risks they accept while on the road.

ENVIRONMENTAL RISK

Environmental Risk is the risk which exists as a result of the environment we ride in. They are the big "what ifs" and should give the rider pause before rolling out of the driveway. Every time a rider throws a leg over a motorcycle, the rider faces risks that cannot be immediately specified and yet may be reasonably envisioned. Most of these risks will never be seen or appreciably noticed on a ride, but instead of waiting for these risks to loom large, the rider can begin to mentally account for them as unknown factors and proceed with appropriate caution regardless of how inappreciable the risk may appear to the unpracticed eye.

On an open country road in the middle of farmland, large animals such as deer are an environmental risk. In the heart of the city, environmental risks include parked cars and pedestrians. Persistently bad pavement, poor visibility, or wet weather are also risks that a rider is likely to encounter at some point regardless of where the ride goes. Any risk that the rider might imagine before throwing a leg over the motorcycle can be described as an environmental risk. They do not present any immediate threat to the rider, but rather a small probability of becoming a danger under unforeseen circumstances.

Each rider will feel particularly comfortable with different risks. The rider whose skills have been honed commuting through a large city will be far more comfortable riding in the rush hour twilight than the rider who sets out only on sunny summer days. The rider of country roads will be more familiar with the dangers that frequently present themselves in those situations, such as slow-moving farm implements, deer, or gravel on the roadway.

Environmental risks are countless and in some cases unimaginable. When the rider identifies them as a real hazard, they can be classified as situational risks. And, as these risks become critical in importance, they become tactical risks.

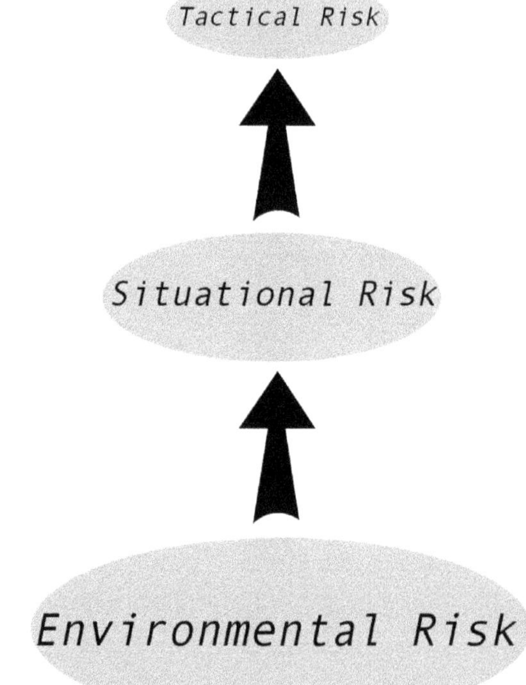

Although environmental risks exist in the abstract, the evaluation of environmental risks does not stop when the rider leaves the driveway; it is an ongoing activity. Whenever situations change, no matter how minutely, the rider must undertake a reevaluation of these environmental risks. The following factors in this section provide a partial list of the considerations that a rider should weigh when determining the risks that may be present on a particular ride.

Where to Ride

Every locale and type of road presents unique hazards. Freeways tend to have higher speeds, higher traffic densities, and fewer places to safely turn off or stop. Forest roads are full of animals and wet leaves and tend to be curvy, which inhibits forward visibility. Farmland roads are often straight and could be conducive to high speed travel if not for the presence of slow-moving machinery and enough food to sustain a large wildlife population. Mountain roads present hazards such as steep drop-offs, rock slides, and gravel. Riding near shopping centers, scenic locales, and cities increase the risk of encountering drivers paying attention to distractions or making aggressive and surprising maneuvers to get where they need to go. Even at times when there may not be other traffic in sight, the mere presence of parking lot exits, driveways, and cross streets all play a part in determining a safe speed- each of these greatly increases the possibility of other cars "coming out of nowhere".

When to ride

Certain times of the day are prime times for pedestrians, such as adults walking around or children playing, while certain times of night are prime time for drunks to be stumbling out into the street or driving home. If a rider is traveling through a forest or famland at the times that deer or other wild animals prefer to feed, there is additional environmental risk there as well. Traveling past ballparks during the season or malls on the weekend are also opportunities for riders to encounter an unusual number of hazardous situations.

Traffic Conditions

Rush hour raises the traffic density to its peak and people leaving work aren't always in the most pleasant or polite of moods, so aggressive driving becomes more common. A rider would be wise to take this frequent aggression into consideration when deciding how to interact with traffic, but even the most casual driving scenarios present special risks. Whereas rush hour drivers mostly know how to get where they are going, Sunday drivers are typically traveling places that they do not go every day. The reduced congestion encourages higher speeds, but a larger percentage of the drivers are inevitably confused about how to reach their destination; slamming brakes, last-second turns, and crossing multiple lanes of traffic becomes a more common occurrence.

Weather

All types of weather present their own hazards. Even sunshine on a beautiful day can temporarily blind drivers and wash out a motorcycle's headlight when approaching a car with the sun at the rider's back. Darkness also presents dangers as visual acuity is greatly reduced and many drivers and riders remain unaware of how greatly darkness can affect how they see (see chapter 6). Cold days present the risk of hypothermia and may cause the rider to have difficulty operating the controls as quickly as when the body is warm. Hot days increase the risk of dehydration, a very serious concern on a motorcycle, and rainy days exacerbate the cold and also reduce visibility and traction.

Riders should also keep in mind

when dealing with inclement weather that it isn't just the motorcyclist's ability to handle the weather, but also the capabilities of the other drivers and their ability to contend with the motorcyclist's capabilities. While a motorcycle may lose less capability in wet weather, a greater safety margin is still necessary due to the risks presented by surrounding traffic. For example, a rider may find that other vehicles prefer to match the speed of the motorcycle rather than actively selecting their own speeds for the conditions, thereby creating additional risk for the motorcyclist.

Road conditions

Every day and with every season, the roads change. Sand, gravel, road salt, and oil all can be found on roads at varying times, offering reduced and unpredictable traction. For northern riders, freeze-thaw cycles create new potholes throughout the winter, which aren't always patched by the time riding season comes around and they get worse as more traffic travels over them.

Although motorcycles are less affected by rain, they are more affected by gravel, oil, sand, and other debris in the roadway. While the motorcyclist must ride cautiously through this debris, it cannot be forgotten that cars are less affected by it. Therefore, a motorcycle braking for an oily or sandy surface may appear overly cautious and unpredictable to the driver behind.

EXERCISE

Think about the environment you ride in. What unique risks do you face riding where you do? What warnings would you give to another rider making his first trip out into the places that you routinely ride?

Riding Partners

Group riding can be extremely hazardous for the unwary rider. Different riders have different personalities and when they get together, these personalities mix and form a certain group dynamic. Ideally, these groups are supportive and promote safe riding. However, this is not always the case.

Aggressive groups may encourage riders to push beyond their abilities. Some groups may head to the bar and promote the consumption of alcohol before and during rides. Other groups may consist of many inexperienced riders, which can place even an experienced rider at considerable risk. Even cautious groups of new riders place each other at greater risk of danger due to their collective inexperience.

Physical Factors

There are also physical factors such as medicines that may cause drowsiness, impair judgment, or cause side effects which are not conducive to riding. Alcohol impairs judgment and reduces reaction time. Even over-the-counter substances such as cigarettes and cold medications can cause very dangerous impairments (Chapter 6).

STRATEGIES FOR COPING WITH ENVIRONMENTAL RISK

Because environmental risks exist in the abstract, they are controlled by the broader decisions riders make with two of the key factors being mental awareness and speed selection.

The rider's ability to continually assess changing situations is crucial. Anything which distracts from a constant assessment and reassessment will contribute to increased exposure to environmental risk. Distractions such as work, grocery lists, children, and significant others can limit a rider's ability or willingness to focus on the important matters pertaining to the ride. The simplest approach to increasing awareness of environmental risk include taking unplanned breaks as necessary, stopping for food, changing clothes to maintain comfort, and spending ample time off the bike to critically assess changes in riding situations and avoiding riding when unusually distracted or tired.

Riders cannot avoid occasional mental distractions; they are an inevitable part of life. While it is obvious that a rider should decline to ride while severely distracted, slight distractions will occasionally creep in during a ride. Riders can cope with distractions by allowing themselves additional time to devote to the task of riding by slowing down.

GET-THERE-ITIS

Get-there-itis multiplies the dangers of every risk a rider faces. It occurs when riders place the destination ahead of the journey by taking short cuts, chances, and making dubious decisions that they would not have made under better circumstances.

Think about this: being in a hurry takes years off your riding experience. Every skill, technique, and habit you have has been developed over the years you've been riding. You have instincts that have been carefully honed and work almost flawlessly as you ride; you don't even have to think about it. Deep down you know why you do not cut corners, why you don't take off from a light without carefully looking in all directions, and why you don't take particular chances that might save you a few precious seconds.

By riding the way you always ride, your conscious and subconscious work together to keep you safe; it's business as usual on the bike as you ride safely day-in and day-out the same way you always have. However, when you press yourself to save precious seconds, you ride differently. All those habits and techniques that have become ingrained over the years are cast aside and by discarding this wealth of experience, you force your subconscious to learn a new system of riding and staying safe. When you ride with a different system, you become a new rider all over again with the same old lessons lurking ahead, waiting to be relearned.

Although time continually moves forward, speed is adjustable. Regardless of the distraction, riders have the ability to control the speed at which most hazards present themselves and the speed at which they approach the hazard. By selecting a lower speed or increasing following distance, a rider can create additional time to respond to most hazards.

The task of speed selection should never result in a single invariable number. Instead, it should be a range of speeds for the conditions that arise from moment to moment. At the high end of the range, speed selection is based on environmental risks such as weather, likely traffic conditions, and time of day. The low end of the range is based on the prevalence of situational and tactical risks which force motorists to actively respond to dangerous situations and frequently requires cautionary or emergency braking.

A motorcyclist who reduces speed and refuses to push beyond personal limits, whether mental, physical or external, will have the best chance at minimizing the dangers of environmental risks. Whether the number placed on the rider's speedometer is regulated by speed limits on an open freeway or common sense on an icy back road, the rider will decide, whether consciously or not, the speed at which to travel. It is, of course, best to think about it consciously and apply logic to the decision.

SITUATIONAL RISK

Situational risks can be thought of as environmental risks starting to look ugly; they are actively developing situations. With hundreds of vehicles parked along the street, it is the car with the lights on, the driver with a seatbelt on, a turning wheel, or some other subtle cue that turns an environmental risk into a situational risk.

Anything that triggers the rider's attention and diverts the rider's focus has become a situational risk; a deer or pedestrian identified as a possible hazard, a car coming upon a red light too fast for comfort or waiting to turn left as the light turns yellow.

Situational risks can be divided into two categories: static and dynamic

Situational risks can be divided into two categories: static and dynamic. Static situational risks are ones which do not move: pot holes, gravel, ice, and oil are static risks. Deer, pedestrians, and other vehicles are dynamic situational risks; they may move along with you, thwarting any attempt at avoiding them. Dynamic situational hazards are clearly the most challenging because they may require the rider to change avoidance strategies on the fly. A timely and easily-managed swerve to the left to avoid a car pulling out of a parallel parking spot may become a panicked swerve to the right when the rider realizes the driver is actually making a U-turn in the middle of the street. This is where the concept of maintaining presence and escape routes becomes crucial.

STRATEGIES FOR COPING WITH SITUATIONAL RISK

There are two strategies for coping with situational risk. The first is maintaining a high degree of presence. The second is maintaining escape routes.

A rider's presence is the ability to be perceived by others, usually through a combination of visibility and audibility. Pedestrians and drivers, perhaps even deer, are less inclined to jump out into traffic when they are aware a vehicle is around. Maximizing factors that allow a rider to be perceived will increase the chance that other drivers, pedestrians and even animals will assist the rider in safely reaching the destination. Too often riders say that another driver did not see them, but the astute rider takes responsibility for this and actively seeks out ways to be

EXERCISE

Come up with a list of about 10 situational risks that you encounter regularly while riding. How can you identify these risks while they are farther up the road? How can you respond to them more quickly?

perceived.

Wearing brightly-colored gear, including a helmet, will help a rider to be seen. Also, using the high beams during the daytime helps increase visibility and is not as distracting to other traffic as it would be at night.

Multiple escape routes multiply the rider's chance of survival

Another way to increase visibility is to position the motorcycle where it can easily be seen before beginning to pass or enter locations which are likely to contain situational risks. For example, motorcyclists can often peer through the window of a parked car to assess when it is safe to pull out into a busy intersection, but in doing so, how visible is the rider to oncoming traffic? Riders would be better advised to pull forward, nearly out into the intersection, making their body and the side of the motorcycle fully visible to other traffic before pulling out.

When traveling down the road, lane selection also plays a large factor in determining how visible a rider will be to others. Considering where other drivers' mirrors are pointed and where they are likely to look can also help in selecting positions that assist others in perceiving the rider's presence.

Another method for being perceived is the use of loud pipes or a loud horn. Loud pipes offend many even when they are not actively preventing hazardous situations. A better option is the use of an aftermarket horn to blast away at the most crucial moments and can freeze pedestrians, motorists and other hazards dead in their tracks. Loud horns are cheap to purchase, easy to retrofit, and allow the rider to grab more attention at key moments. By contrast, loud pipes are quieter and always on, failing to give drivers warning as to when a situation has truly become hazardous for a rider.

The second strategy for mitigating situational risk is maintaining escape routes. As a vehicle threatens to pull out and take away the rider's ability to stop or

Situational risk is common in offroading. The lower speeds prevent a lot of surprises, but managing your way through rough terrain requires the rider to plan ahead.

swerve, maneuvering options become limited. It is the loss of these maneuvering options and the challenge of regaining them that is the central theme around which many strategies for safer street riding can be developed.

Oft-repeated words of wisdom pertaining to dynamic situational risk include, "ride like you're invisible" or "ride like they're out to get you". While these suggestions may foster a healthy paranoiac mindset, this book presents a more practical bit of advice that offers, not just a mindset, but also a recommendation with practical applications: Never Relinquish Your Escape Routes!

Multiple escape routes multiply the rider's chances of survival. Chapter 4, idscusses the four escape routes: swerve right, swerve left, brake, and accelerate. Ideally, any hazardous situation can be averted by any of the four methods. However, as a practical matter, it is unlikely in most situations that more than

The rider encountering this hazard at a leisurely pace faced a situational risk in deciding how to get around it. Certainly, this would be no problem while traveling at a reasonable speed. However, face the same situation at elevated speeds and the need for decisive braking or swerving certainly qualifies this as a tactical risk.

EXERCISE

Knowing that high-performance riding skills can save your life or prevent a nasty accident, how confident are you in your riding skills? In what areas can you improve? How can you practice these skills safely?

two, or perhaps three, will bring a rider to safety. Knowing this, the rider facing situational risks will evaluate the four escape routes and strive to retain as many of them as possible. Adjust course and speed to ensure that at least two escape routes remain open for the entire duration of any situational hazard.

The most commonly surrendered escape route is that of acceleration. If a rider is already traveling at what feels like the maximum safe speed for conditions, then the rider has effectively surrendered a quarter of the potential maneuvering options. Riding outside of the comfort level, even momentarily, increases the rider's risk. For this reason, maintaining an amount of speed in reserve can provide a much safer ride, leaving the option open for the rider to accelerate out of trouble without exceeding personal limits. It should also be noted that maintaining some reserve speed is also a good strategy for avoiding law enforcement citations.

Riders also surrender escape routes when they fall into a group of vehicles and cease to think about the entirety of their actions for themselves. If each motorist got onto an empty freeway, they would select the speed that they felt was reasonable for them. However, all too often, a faster vehicle passes a slower one and the slower vehicle suddenly matches the others' speed and in so doing. the two motorists have managed to inadvertently placed two independently controlled large metal objects, traveling at high speed, in close proximity. Certainly a rider should not trust an anonymous driver sitting in the rider's safety zone and, similarly, riders should be wary of anyone into whose safety zone the they have entered.

When traveling down a busy freeway, drivers and riders are especially prone to visually latch onto the vehicle in front of them and depend on the vehicle ahead to turn at each curve in the road and to brake at the appropriate time. The only description for this type of behavior is carelessness and the only explanation for it is laziness. Each motorist should select the speed that they feel is reasonable and each rider should avoid letting other vehicles latch onto them, just as they should avoid latching onto other vehicles.

To avoid losing a part of the safety zone when another vehicle latches on, a rider may decide to slow down, use the bike's acceleration to put some quick distance between the motorcycle and the offending vehicle, or change lanes. Generally, very gradual adjustments to speed or position are ineffective, tending to encourage the other vehicle to follow along. A sharp and decisive move is far more likely to jolt the person out of their trance and force them to reassess the speed at which they wish to be traveling. Of course, some drivers will view it as a challenge and try to match the motorcycle's speed regardless of what the rider does. If a rider's personal safety margins and speed limits do not permit getting away from this driver, it may be best to simply take a break rather than ride alongside someone who is known to be deliberately maintaining close proximity.

In the upcoming chapters 3 and 4, further detail will be provided with strategies for maintaining escape routes.

TACTICAL RISK

Tactical Risk is situational risk that presents a clear danger to the motorcyclist such as a car turning into the path of the motorcycle, a deer caught dangerously close in the headlights, or gravel in mid-turn. Tactical risks demand immediate and precise reaction.

All experienced riders have encountered a variety of sweat-inducing and heart-pounding moments of danger, but for every such moment, there have undoubtedly been countless moments where attentive riding prevented such

The techniques for emergency braking, swerving, and braking while turning do not come naturally. They must be learned and practiced in a safe and controlled environment.

Riders on the street should remain diligent in ensuring that the skills needed for coping with tactical risks remain both frequently practiced and seldom used

danger. Successful riders are able to avoid tactical risks most of the time. As a result, if riders only focus on crashes or tactical risks when assessing their riding, they miss out on the vast majority of lessons to be learned. That is why this chapter started out with environmental and strategic risks; they are the day-to-day experiences that riders encounter on a regular basis. They provide the greatest opportunity to learn about avoiding tactical risk. The good street riders are those who face environmental and situational risks with aplomb and rarely allow them to rise to the level of becoming tactical risks. Nevertheless, from time to time, those sweat-inducing and heart-pounding moments arise. These tactical risks color every aspect of motorcycling. They are manageable in most situations, but they are most assuredly best avoided.

STRATEGIES FOR COPING WITH TACTICAL RISK

The skills necessary for coping with tactical risks are nearly the same on the public street as they are on the race track although the dangers are quite different. The hazards of street riding are unique and far less predictable, requiring careful consideration by the rider.

When considering hazards such as oil and water on the roadway, bad

Yellow road signs provide cautionary information. Oftentimes, recommended speeds are posted on entrance ramps and sharp curves. Be aware that each state sets these recommendations differently. In some states, it may be safe to double the posted recommendation in a well-maintained vehicle. In other states, just a few miles per hour over the recommendation may result in catastrophe. These signs do not have a national standard and it would be foolish to assume you can use these as a benchmark to determine how fast you can take an unknown curve.

pavement, grit and gravel, bad tires, less than optimal brakes, etc., it is easy to imagine just how much maneuvering ability, braking ability, and acceleration is commonly surrendered by riders on public roads. These hazards eat directly into the rider's safety margin when dealing with a tactical risk and is the reason why practicing emergency maneuvers is even more crucial for street riders. Riders on the street should remain diligent in ensuring that the skills needed for coping with tactical risks remain both frequently practiced and seldom used.

Always remember that tactical risks are more varied on the street than on a track. Oncoming cars, vehicles making left-hand turns, sudden stops for no apparent reason, cell phone talkers; none of these hazards exist on a track. On a track, everybody is going the same direction with 100% focus and seeking the same objective. The reality on the street could not be more different.

In addition to the usual track-riding skills that can save a rider who is facing tactical risk, one skill that takes on added importance is the ability to adjust for, or avoid, evolving tactical risks. For example, a car slamming on its brakes appears as a straight-forward hazard. It would be easy enough to swerve to the left or to the right, perhaps emergency brake, in order to avoid the risk. However, often it is not that

SPEED LIMITS

Speed limits are set by statute, creating a maximum legal speed on the road. At one time in America's history, speed limits were based upon safety, helping motorists maintain safe speeds in unfamiliar areas. Nowadays, speed limits are as likely to be set for political reasons or fuel economy reasons. At times, they are even set arbitrarily. Nevertheless, the laws are enforced to varying degrees and strict compliance is the best policy if you are not familiar with the area in which you are traveling or the reasons why the limits were set how they were.

Yellow speed limit signs are cautionary, often used for unusually tight curves or areas which present unique hazards. Although the yellow signs are not mandatory, it is important to remember that each jurisdiction may set their recommendations for different reasons. In some areas it may be possible to significantly exceed the recommendation under ideal conditions, but this is not always the case. When traveling in an unfamiliar area, be careful to take the posted recommendations very seriously as the cause for the recommended speed may not be immediately apparent.

simple. The fact that the driver is slamming on his brakes may indicate he is about to turn right. Or left. Or back up. When facing risks dealing with other people, the rider must remember that they are likely to change course unpredictably. One type of tactical risk may quickly evolve into another and each time the risk changes, the rider has less time than before to react.

The odds of a rider escaping an evolved tactical risk are directly proportional to the number of escape routes that the rider has available to choose from. For example, the stopping car scenario may evolve into a right turn or left turn. If the rider facing the tactical risk of being unable to brake hard enough decides to swerve, there's a fifty-fifty chance that there will be a bad outcome., depending on which way the car turns.

In addition to the braking car, there are a number of other moments of tactical uncertainty that present hazardous situations. Some of these situations include the following: drivers creeping out into an intersection who may go straight, or turn right or left; a car parked on the side of the road who may pull out, open their door, or make a U-turn; a swerving car which may be beginning to turn, swerving to turn the other direction, or may be on a cell phone or be drunk and do who-knows-what.

Riders can "cheat" tactical risk through experience. They can develop an intuition based on very subtle cues which help them select the right escape route when forced to choose. However, no rider is immune to the risk. When dealing with probability, the odds will eventually win. It is best to avoid tactical risks altogether, perhaps taking it somewhere safer, a race track, where everybody is going in the same direction and paying attention.

RELATIVE SPEED

Relative speed is a factor in many collisions. For example, the relative speed between the motorcycle and a car traveling in the same direction at the same speed will be zero, meaning the car and motorcycle will never cross paths if they continue to travel at the same speed and direction. Ideally, all vehicles on a road would travel at the same speed and in the same direction. Under these circumstances, the risk of vehicles crossing paths, and therefore the risk of a collision, is minimized. By contrast, additional care and attention must be paid wherever vehicles are likely to be traveling at different directions or at different speeds, such as in the presence of intersections or highly-traveled roads.

ANGEROUS POSITIONS 2

While chapter 1 focused on the general concept of risk, this chapter focuses more on very detailed and specific risks. Just like those presented already, these hazards can be categorized as environmental, situational, or tactical. However, the frequency with which these specific situations arise justify additional consideration by the rider.

The following seven situations are strategic risks that will very likely evolve into tactical risks for every rider at some point during their riding career. These seven situations can best be described as common, frequently insignificant, and best avoided. Staying safe on the street requires riders actively maneuver against even low-probability events with a high degree of consistency.

SITUATION ONE- The Blind Spot

The blind spot is commonly the result of poorly-aligned side view mirrors. Cars with side view mirrors angled to the rear rather than the sides will have a blind spot along their rear quarter-panel, extending out and to the back.

Due to the hazards present whenever a rider is in proximity to other vehicles and the increased risk whenever a rider's presence is not known, the blind spot is a very dangerous place for a rider to remain. Adjusting the throttle position, applying the brakes, or maneuvering to minimize time spent in a vehicle's blind spot is a sure way to decrease risk while riding.

Riding in another vehicle's blind spot is dangerous for two reasons. First, the rider is effectively invisible to the other car. Second, it takes maneuvering ability away from the motorcycle as well as the car- by sitting just off the rear quarter panel or bumper, the rider is effectively blocking the driver in, increasing the risk of being involved in an accident. Unfortunately, motorcyclists often make a good crumple zone for cars facing emergency situations because, if forced to choose, drivers will be better off colliding with a motorcyclist than with

Properly adjusted side view mirrors will show a driver who is to their side, but all too often these mirrors are grossly misadjusted, being angled toward the rear of the vehicle. Approach with caution!

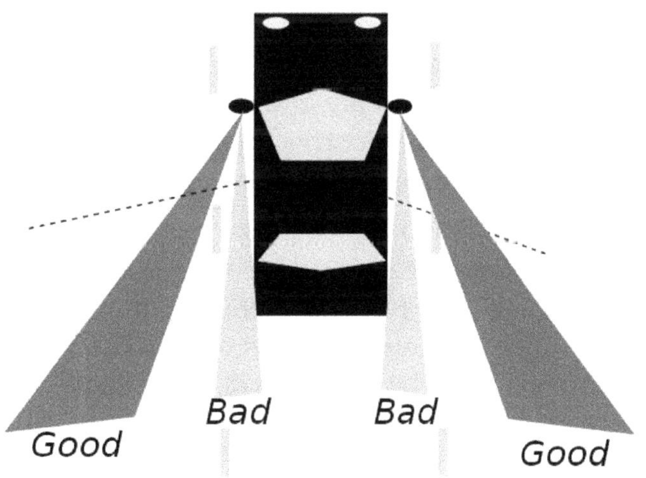

The surest sign of improperly adjusted side view mirrors is that you are able to see the driver's face when behind them in the same lane, but not when alongside them. This is your sign to twist the throttle, squeeze the brake, or do whatever else you can to get away as it is reasonably certain the driver is not aware of your presence.

The fact that you can see this driver's face in the side view mirror from behind almost guarantees that, once you are alongside him, he will not be able to see you. Also, the construction cone blocking the rear view doesn't instill confidence in his common sense either.

virtually any other obstacle on the road. By keeping out of the car's blind spot and as far away as possible, riders decrease the likelihood that someone will use their motorcycle as a crumple zone.

Due to improperly adjusted mirrors, the blind spot can extend across more than a single lane. On a wide highway, a rider can be two lanes over and still be in a driver's blind spot. The likelihood of encountering a multiple lane change increases whenever there is a change in traffic density and drivers feel compelled to aggressively jockey for a better position without first checking their mirrors.

SITUATION TWO- Entrance/Exit Ramps and Merging

Merging is one of the most challenging and stressful tasks routinely performed by motorists. It involves a change in speed and direction with only a brief moment available to familiarize oneself with the new road. For merging motorcyclists, the best advice is to plan the merging strategy as early as possible. Knowing the traffic density and speed in advance and also being certain to visually check for road conditions and hazards on the ramp itself as early as possible minimizes possible surprises during a merge. Being leaned over on a ramp while accelerating and turning around to survey traffic conditions is a terrible time to discover a shredded tire or an odd wash of gravel across the road's surface.

The most seamless way to merge with traffic is to get up to the speed of the other traffic, or even a little bit faster, and maintain a steady speed in preparation for the merge. Traveling at a slightly higher rate of speed has the effect of keeping traffic moving toward the rider from the front, rather than creeping up from behind.

For viewing vehicles to the rear, the rider's mirrors will likely be ineffective due to the angle at which the motorcycle merges. This is made worse when the

Another time to be be distrustful of mirrors is while passing cars parked along the side of the street. Drivers seldom check their mirrors before opening their doors and may of fling them open without regard for who may be approaching from behind.

When entrance or exit ramps contain a curve, your lean angle reduces the effectiveness of your mirrors. For this and many other reasons, it is crucial for riders to keep their "heads on a swivel", actively looking around with all their vision, rather than relying on the tiny vibrating mirrors that only provide a limited picture of the surroundings.

motorcycle is leaned over, such as going through a cloverleaf. Turning around and even adjusting body position can help the rider to survey the situation to the rear. The stability of the motorcycle at speed will allow an experienced rider to twist around, even changing position on the seat, to easily look over either shoulder. This is especially important because, even with the majority of traffic traveling slower and appearing to approach the rider from the front, there is always the possibility that a single faster vehicle may be approaching quickly from the rear as the rider merges.

Sometimes drivers will make the mistake of coming to a stop on entrance ramps and patiently wait for an opening. On some ramps, especially during construction activities or on poorly designed roads, this is the expected behavior. Other times, it is done simply because the driver does not feel comfortable merging into the traffic. If a rider encounters someone stopping on a ramp or merging zone, hopefully it was spotted well in advance, otherwise it will come as an unwelcome surprise as the rider travels down the ramp expecting to merge at speed. Even if the driver does not come to a complete stop, a decision to slow down will make things more difficult. These slow merges create a significant risk of being rear-ended after entering the roadway and also pose a risk to anyone else who follows down the entrance ramp expecting to merge at speed.

Merging isn't just dangerous for the person merging. As a rider on the freeway approaching a merging point, verify that all options are available: braking, accelerating, and changing lanes. A slow car attempting to merge may pull out aggressively and force a rider to apply the brakes, move into another lane, or accelerate past. It is generally considered courteous and advisable, to move over to another lane to assist other vehicles that are merging. Be aware though that being farther away isn't always safe either, as a merging vehicle may move over multiple lanes without clearing the way.

While riding on a freeway, remember that merging is stressful for other drivers. Expect the unexpected and try to anticipate any need to leave the lane or change course to accommodate other motorists.

Ever think you'd be dodging a 19 foot sail boat on the interstate?

SITUATION THREE- Behind Large Trucks or Utility Vehicles

The most valuable information a rider receives comes from the ability to see far down the road. Backing off and giving the vehicle ahead extra space makes it easier for the rider to see around them and farther up the road. The larger the vehicle, the more crucial this extra vision will be. Who knows how many pedestrians, how much cross-traffic, and how many other hazards in the road the rider may suddenly be able to see when the view is no longer obstructed.

By maintaining better vision down the road, riders can also gain an advantage by looking for brake lights farther ahead. Each motorist needs about 0.4 seconds to react and apply the brakes. So if a rider can see brake lights far up ahead, either by looking around or through the car in front, the rider can obtain valuable advance warning of a slow-down ahead. This is especially valuable on the highway. By looking just one more car ahead, the rider will have an extra four-tenths of a second to react. Further more, if the rider can see all the way down the road, ten, twenty, thirty cars ahead, that may equate to up to 12 seconds or more of advanced warning and this can vastly improve a rider's chances of safely coming to a stop. However, when the rider cannot see past the truck or SUV in front, this important information is lost.

Another hazard, related to large trucks and utility vehicles concerns the items they may be carrying. A pickup truck may be transporting just about anything in its bed and its cargo can often be obscured behind the tailgate. The rider may have no way of knowing what is

.there, let alone whether it is safely tied down. I can personally attest to mattresses and ladders bouncing into the middle of the road.

Gravel flying out from construction vehicles and debris from trucks heading to the dump are another concern. Vehicles with larger tires also tend to throw more rocks up from the road and into the path of other motorists.

Trailers have also been known to come unhitched from time to time. Ever think you'd be dodging a 19 foot sailboat on the interstate? Small and large trailers alike sway back and forth on a bad tire or in windy conditions and they are not always safely under the control of the inexperienced drivers who may be driving just as fast as they would without the trailer attached. With all these potential hazards, it is not an exaggeration to say that the more you ride, the more ingrained the habit will become of staying away from anything that's carrying anything anywhere.

SITUATION FOUR- In Proximity to Any Vehicle Which Is Slowing or Stopping

Often drivers get confused, start to slow down or turn, and suddenly realize they've made a mistake. Then it is all too common for them to maneuver rapidly to get back where they "should be" without regard for other traffic that may have begun to pass them by. The most common heads-up for a rider should be when a vehicle slows down multiple times. Whether a sign of being intoxicated, lost, distracted, or clueless, they are not the vehicle to take any chances with. Brake lights are a valuable indicator, not only of reduced speed, but also of unpredictable behavior to come. Whenever a vehicle starts to slow down or comes to a stop in an unusual location- even if it's just a brief tap of a brake light- riders should slow down and back off, never presuming to know what the driver is doing.

On a crowded street, a rider might see someone turning into a parallel parking spot, only to see him emerge a second later to make a U-turn directly through the rider's path. It is crucial, when encountering a slowing vehicle, to avoid guessing what is likely to happen and instead try to imagine what might happen under the worst case scenario. Don't assume that brake lights illuminating before an intersection indicate the driver's intention to casually turn at the next street instead of aggressively braking to turn into the seldom-used driveway 40 feet before it or stopping in the middle of the street altogether to drop off a loved one in front of a building.

Never presume to know what a

slowing or stopping vehicle is going to do next. Always approach and pass with extreme caution.

This is not the time to discover that the driver in front of you wants to make a U-turn, or that he missed his turn and will be coming to an immediate stop and will use reverse to back up. It is also a bad time for the driver in front of you to discover that an over-sized soft drink doesn't fit in the cup holder, or that his wife wants a divorce. Unfortunately, there is no way to know what is about to happen while you are following too closely.

SITUATION FIVE– Approaching an Accident or Any Other Distraction

After an accident, the ensuing traffic jam might best be described as orderly group of citizens waiting patiently in line to view the carnage. As hard as it might be, riders must practice keeping their focus on the road ahead and on the surrounding motorists because those other motorists most assuredly are not doing the same. The attentive rider actively avoids creating a second accident, rather than struggling to catch a glimpse of the first. This is a skill that must be practiced, be it an accident, a video billboard, or an altercation at a bus stop. The more something catches the rider's eye, the more certainly it has caught the eyes of others as well. The harder it is to resist the urge to look, the more crucial it is that riders do just that.

Other distractions during which riders can predict unusual and dangerous behavior includes scenic areas, anywhere with a crowd of people, fireworks, and any vehicle approaching with flashing lights.

Brake lights are a valuable indicator, not only of reduced speed, but also of unpredictable behavior to come

WATCHING FOR BRAKE LIGHTS

In heavy traffic with small following distances, a driver can slam on his brakes and cause a rear-end collision. Riders can reduce the chances of such a collision by looking far down the road to anticipate when other vehicles will begin braking.

On a road, each car will have to stop or slow for the same hazards and reasons. Therefore, long before the car in front of you touches the brakes, many cars far ahead are already using theirs. Watching for brake lights in the distance gives a rider advance warning, serving as a signal to the rider to cover the brake, increase following distance, and prepare to slow down. Other indicators that cars are likely to stop include: stop signs and lights, parking lots, hazard markings in the road (signs intended to slow traffic or reroute vehicles in an unfamiliar manner), and anything that looks interesting such as an accident on the side of the road, flashing lights, or a gathering of people. When riders recognize these attention traps, they must remain focused even as surrounding drivers become more distracted.

SITUATION SIX- Oncoming Vehicles

On a two-lane road, an oncoming car can cross the center line into the rider's lane in under a second. It is simply a matter of covering the 6 to 8 feet of lateral distance. Combine the high closing speed of oncoming traffic with the short distance they must cover to collide with a rider and it is easy to see how oncoming traffic can pose an enormous risk.

When a vehicle is approaching, it is hard to judge their speed and almost impossible to tell whether they are accelerating or slowing down. The brake lights cannot be seen from the front and from a distance it may be exceedingly difficult to see the nose of a car dive down under heavy braking or rise under acceleration.

The difficulty of identifying cues from oncoming traffic makes it hard for riders to spot drivers who are about to change course and turn into oncoming traffic. The best way to combat this problem is to be seen. Assuming the rider has done everything possible to enhance visibility, such as activating the high beams and selecting optimal lane positioning, there are not many additional options left to the rider. Clearly a rider cannot slow down for every oncoming car. However, there are small steps the rider can take to identify when this risk is more likely to occur and other steps that riders can take to momentarily enhance the motorcycle's visibility.

With the lack of available visual information, more subtle cues must be seized by the rider to obtain hints regarding upcoming dangers from oncoming traffic. One such warning sign is a long line of cars. The long line increases the odds that one of the cars will want to turn. In addition, there is an increased risk that one of the cars toward the back is growing impatient and may decide to move aggressively out into the oncoming lane either to pass or else to take out their aggression through a fast turn onto another road or parking lot.

Another warning sign is a change in lane position. Many drivers telegraph their intentions, often swerving slightly within their lane before turning. Therefore, any side-to-side movement may indicate a pending turn or an inattentive driver who may swerve into your lane. Another thing to look for would be the driver's face, if possible. You may see where the driver is looking and it may indicate a possible change in direction.

When encountering a vehicle which poses a risk of turning, swerving, or pulling out into the rider's lane, one option is to move to the other side of the lane, or across lanes, away from the oncoming traffic. This serves two purposes: the lateral movement in the swerve makes the motorcycle instantly more visible, exposing the broad side of the motorcycle, and it also takes the rider farther away from the oncoming car. Taking the swerve a step farther, another strategy is to swerve within the lane, moving left-to-right-to-left and so on. As previously stated, swerving side to side increases the rider's visibility. It also tends to place doubt into the minds of surrounding drivers, encouraging them to pause and exercise additional caution in order to ascertain the rider's intentions. Finally, in traffic conditions such as these, a rider may be better off in the company of other cars as a pack will be easily seen. However, this comes with its own set of risks due to the loss of maneuvering options.

SITUATION SEVEN- Areas of Invisibility

While it is often said that motorcyclists should not rely on other vehicles seeing them, it is also true that there are times when a motorcyclist truly cannot be seen. Riders should practice the utmost caution in these situations and do their best to remedy them through intelligent use of lane positioning.

When approaching an intersection, a rider must be careful to keep sight lines open to all lanes of traffic, ensuring that the motorcycle and rider are not obscured by other vehicles. If a rider cannot see a lane of traffic, it is reasonable to assume that the traffic will not perceive the rider. In these cases, it is imperative to actively seek better lane positions and vehicle spacings to ensure recognition by other drivers or else slow down to a speed that permits more radical maneuvering. The following are three common situations in which a rider and automobile will be obscured from each other, with the potential for disastrous results.

With everyone stopped, it only seems natural to pull up on the right to pass, but the angle prevents you from seeing oncoming cars attempting to turn into the driveway on the right.

this image, you are waiting to turn left ce the oncoming SUV also turns left. hat you cannot see is the car about 25 ds behind the SUV in the right lane.

The truck in the background is turning right. That means, coming from the other direction, there are four vehicles hidden from view. While a semi truck offers the possibility of seeing vehicles underneath it, the van does an even better job of hiding critical information from the rider. Keep your eyes open, looking for places for cars to hide and you will find that the possibilities are plentiful. Below, you can see a nearly identical scenario from the other side.

INTERSECTIONS 3

THE DANGERS OF INTERSECTIONS

When approaching an intersection, the rider nears a location where a number of motorcycling's greatest hazards are known to congregate. Vehicles changing speed and direction always increase a rider's risk and vehicles all accelerate, brake and turn at intersections. In addition, poor pavement with ripples and crowning due to frequent braking, gravel due to frequent turns, fluids such as oil and coolant from leaks pooling up over time, and painted lines all tend to be more prevalent at intersections. Because of the other vehicles, the rider must pay greater attention when nearing intersections. Vehicles in front may suddenly slam on their brakes to make their turn, vehicles in back may not be ready to slow or stop for a short yellow light, pedestrians may jump out into the street, and the rider's traction may be very limited.

While attempting to cope with the variety of hazards near an intersection, riders will also encounter other cars and trucks. These vehicles may be rather oblivious to the road hazards and even be aggressively jockeying for position so they can get through the light as quickly as possible when it changes. The rider's concerns of road conditions, oil, and debris are not nearly as significant to a stable four-wheeled vehicle. For a motorcyclist, the mental workload may triple at a complicated intersection due to these bike-specific hazards while drivers in cars and trucks couldn't be less aware.

At an intersection, there are a number of potential circumstances that may necessitate the rider taking swift action. Events such as a light changing to yellow, a pedestrian crossing the street, a car making a left turn in front of the rider are just a few possible occurrences which may prevent the rider from crossing the intersection as anticipated. But not only will these events keep the rider from making it through the intersection, they each require the rider to react differently. The challenge of crossing intersections lies not just in the multitude of hazards, but also in the many different responses that a rider may have to make with a split second decision. Under these circumstances, the attentive rider should always be ready to slow down and cover the brake lever for every intersection. In addition, the rider should increase following distances well in advance of any intersection and be certain to look both ways for cross-traffic long before reaching the point where an emergency stop would be necessary.

What follows is a systematic approach in evaluating a variety of the hazards that may be present at an intersection. By evaluating the hazards systematically, riders can work their way through a rapid-fire checklist of possibly life-saving evasive maneuvers.

A typical intersection. Tar snakes, manhole covers, bad pavement, oil, painted lines and arrows, cross traffic, turning traffic, oncoming traffic, cars parked on the sides of the road, plenty of shops, store windows, and signs to distract people, and a high probability of pedestrians. Certainly a place to be careful and attentive.

VEHICLE AVOIDANCE STRATEGIES

A driver turning directly in front of a motorcycle is one of the most dangerous encounters for a rider not just the perceived risk of a collision, but also because a car turning in front of a motorcyclist effectively presents a solid wall for the rider to run into. There may be no sliding across the pavement in such a collision, just a sudden stop jolting tens or even hundreds of G-forces into the rider's body. These types of accidents are statistically among the worst for motorcyclists and the opportunities to avoid them are not always clear. The speed differential between the motorcycle and the turning car and the speed at which a car can get into a motorcyclist's path of travel are always vital concerns.

Some ways to increase visibility include using the high beam during the day time, wearing bright, reflective clothing, and possibly even the use of a brightly colored orange or yellow "construction" vest or a helmet specifically chosen for its eye-catching color. Reflective media with an adhesive backing can also be purchased and applied to helmets, riding gear, luggage, and other parts of the motorcycle. One popular reflective material, shown above, is called Solas®. It is a 3M™ product and is often sold by the roll or by the foot and may be trimmed into different shapes.

Enhancing visibility is a crucial step in preventing other vehicles from crossing the rider's path. One way to capture the attention of other drivers is to join up with a larger group of vehicles. Tucking in closer to another motorcycle or riding in closer proximity to a car allows the rider to ride along in a more visible block of traffic. However, this approach is not without its dangers. Being in the presence of a turning car, with another car alongside, dramatically reduces the rider's escape route options, but many riders deem this to be an acceptable trade-off when traveling through an intersection.

Another option is for the rider to initiate a slight back-and-forth swerve, allowing the lateral movement of the bike and its headlight to attract attention. As the rider reaches the point where a decision must be made to brake or continue on, the rider should stop the swerving, straighten the bike in anticipation of possible braking action, and be prepared for the other vehicle to remain stationary, start to pull out and then stop, or completely attempt to cross the intersection. By this time the rider should have checked whether the other

APPROACHING A LEFT-TURNER

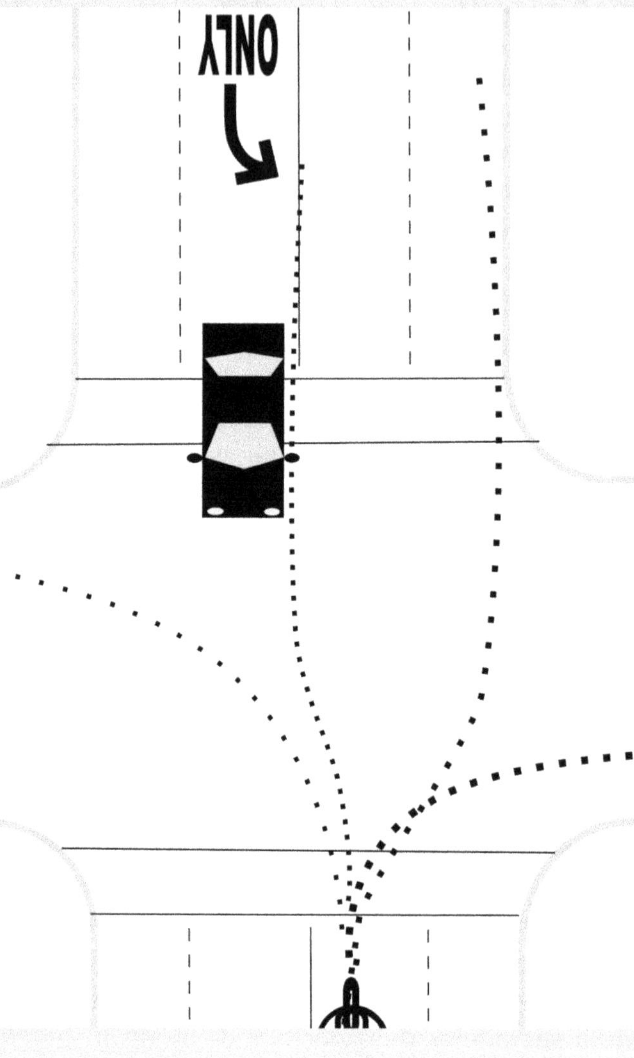

This diagram demonstrates four possible routes around a left-turning vehicle. Which of the paths offers the most successful outcome for the rider depends first on whether the car is determined to complete the turn, or will stop in the lane upon seeing the motorcyclist and whether there is oncoming or crossing traffic.

Regardless of the escape path chosen, the rider's ability to successfully avoid a collision at this stage depends on the ability to maintain target fixation while simultaneously coordinating necessary braking and turning maneuvers.

To gain an appreciation for the complexity of managing intersections, look at the left-most escape path. A left turn is shallower than a turn to the right, so in the event that the driver pulls in front of the rider, it allows the rider to turn at the highest speed- but this can only work for the rider if there is no oncoming traffic. The second escape route, down the center line, might be used when the driver has committed to turning at an impossibly late moment, or suddenly needs to stop across lanes of traffic, being unable to complete the turn. The third escape path is essentially a swerve to avoid the slow-turning car, or a car that starts to turn and then stops upon seeing the motorcyclist. For the right-most escape path, figure out just how slow a rider would have to be going to make such a sharp turn to avoid hitting the car turning in front of the rider's path. Consider the possibility that a sharp right turn may be your only choice if a turning car blocks your entire lane.

Clearly, none of these escape routes will work every time and the rider, having only seconds or less to assess the situation and choose the best path is at a severe disadvantage. These situations are best approached with extreme caution and at an almost exaggeratedly slow speed.

lanes are clear as escape routes, should a swerve into another lane be determined to be the best course of action.

Reducing speed will reduce the severity of any impact, regardless of where it comes from. However, even the act of slowing down could be interpreted by drivers as permission for them to make the turn. Regardless of the strategies employed, intersections will remain one of the greatest hazards for motorcyclists due to the severity and regularity of these crashes.

THE SAFEST ROUTE IN A DANGEROUS SITUATION

It is important to consider that the safest route in a dangerous situation may not be a very desirable route under other circumstances- blowing through an intersection, diving into a driveway or parking lot, or heading for the weeds may be your best option when the alternative is going thirty to zero into the back of a heavy steel cage or facing gravitational acceleration off the side of a cliff. This is where looking far up the road and practicing path visualization comes into play. The farther up the road you've planned, the more time you have to evaluate what might otherwise appear to be an undesireable route.

TRIGGER POINTS

Just as in many other areas of riding, the best way to remain safe is to develop solid riding habits. Trigger points can be used to formalize the process of traversing difficult intersections. The trigger points are two imaginary points on the road leading up to an intersection. They serve as signals, triggering a shift in the rider's attention from one set of hazards in the intersection to the next at the appropriate time.

The first trigger point is the distance at which the rider would normally begin to make a leisurely stop for the intersection. Up until that point, the rider has been largely concerned with the bigger picture of riding. Issues such as following distance and looking far up the road have been the main focus. But after the first trigger point, the rider's attention shifts to the intersection itself.

At the first trigger point, the rider immediately checks the stoplight and begins to cover the brake. If it is yellow or red, the rider begins to stop. Otherwise, the rider begins to plan the route through the intersection by checking for pedestrians crossing the street, cross traffic, and potential left-turning vehicles. The rider maintains focus on these potential hazards until reaching the second trigger point.

The second trigger point is the point at which the rider must begin rapid braking in order to stop before the intersection. At this point, the rider checks the stop light again, ensuring the light is green. If it is not, the rider balances the risk of running through on the yellow light with the risk of being rear-ended should the rider decide to brake hard for the light.

The first trigger point is the point at which a rider begins applying the brake for a leisurely stop. While approaching this point, the rider maintains a normal riding scan and checks the stoplight, determining whether the light is likely to remain green, or if the rider should prepare to stop.

When reaching the first trigger point, the rider rolls off the throttle and covers the brake. If the rider anticipates having to stop, the rider begins braking. If the rider believes it will be possible to pass through the intersection on a green light, the rider shifts scanning techniques from a general riding scan to a more focused scan aimed at identifying intersection-specific hazards such as red light runners, people turning right on red, left-hand turning cars, pedestrians, and hazardous pavement near the intersection. This scan and assessment of present factors should be completed as the rider approaches the second trigger point.

The second trigger point is the last point that a rider can reasonably and safely stop the motorcycle before the intersection. At this point, the rider checks the stop light again, ensuring it is still green.

Past the second trigger point, the rider is in a danger zone where the motorcycle will be incapable of stopping for hazards in the intersection.

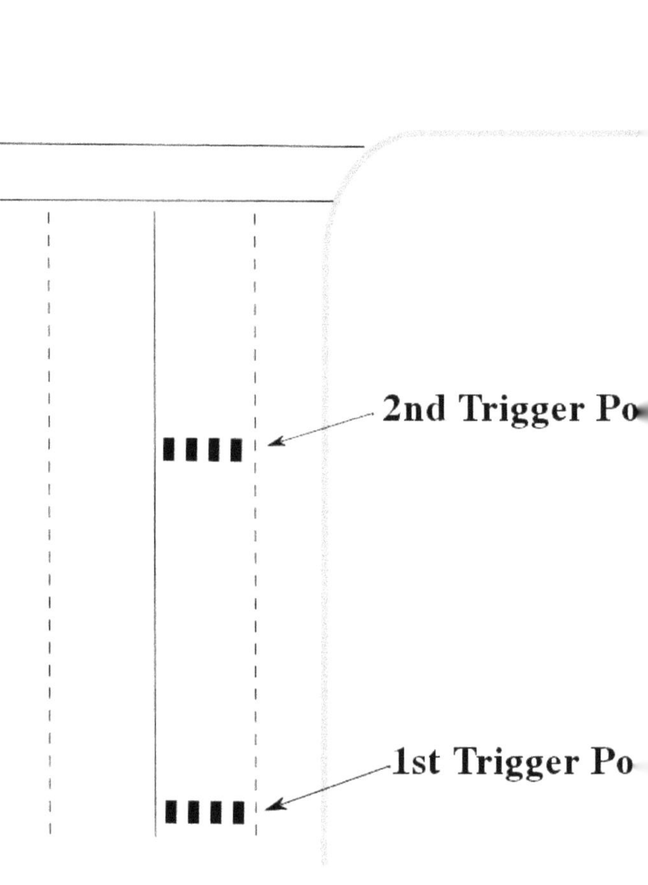

After passing the second trigger point, the rider is now committed to crossing the intersection and will no longer be able to stop for the light. Therefore, past the second trigger point, evasive maneuvers such as swerving, turning, and accelerating take on added importance. This is the point at which intersections become the most dangerous for motorcyclists because only evasive swerving and turning maneuvers within the complex environment of the intersection provide the rider with any chance of escaping a tactical risk. Escape routes attempt to position the rider in a way that the collision, if it occurs, will not be head-on into a vehicle, but rather a glancing blow, allowing the rider to slide or tumble a ways, scrubbing off energy before coming to a stop. Not a pretty picture, indeed. These are the rider's escape options beyond the second trigger point.

FIVE THINGS YOU CAN DO TO AVOID GETTING REAR-ENDED

Activate your brake lights when slowing down, especially while engine braking;

Continue flashing your brake lights once stopped at a light;

Maintain an escape route and watch your rearview mirrors while stopped;

Activate your turn signal far in advance in to provide advance notice and draw attention to your presence;

Make yourself and your motorcycle more visible

TIMING A STREET LIGHT

When stopped at a stop light, the rider should not wait passively for the light to turn green. Positive actions can be taken during this crucial time in order to ensure rider safety. During this period, the most important things to pay attention to are the rear view mirrors and the cars that are waiting to turn left. Keeping an eye on the rear view mirrors is a crucial activity at this point because the most likely collision would be the rider getting rear-ended. Paying attention for vehicles turning left is another critical concern. At any time, the rider might notice a car inching forward, suggesting an aggressive turn when the light turns green, or perhaps a turn signal that flips on momentarily and then gets canceled by an inattentive hand. Any hint the rider can glean which suggests that a left turner may be gunning the light is information worth considering before the light turns green.

When the cross-traffic light turns yellow, the rider has 3 to 6 seconds to run through a crucial checklist. The traffic situation, potentially aggressive drivers, pedestrians, and road conditions must be analyzed before getting underway.

At the moment the light turns yellow, some cars begin speeding up to make it through the intersection, while others begin coming to a stop, and still others may attempt to stop, but fail to do so in time. With experience and practice, a rider can become adept at quickly and accurately identifying which cars are stopping and which ones may not stop in time. During these 3 to 6 seconds, the rider must also look for pedestrians and bicyclists, not just in the intersections, but up the road as well; not everyone crosses at the intersection.

The rider preparing to get underway must also watch for cars turning left. They may be in a left turn lane, but they may also have forgotten to get into the turn lane and may try turning from a middle or even a right lane. And of course, plenty of people forget, or don't bother, to use turn signals so even looking for those signs is a risky bet. Sometimes a rider can look at the driver's face to determine whether they are confused or lost, but at best, whatever information obtained is advisory in nature; it certainly can never be relied upon. A driver thought to be waving someone through an intersection could quite easily be gesturing while on the phone or chasing a bug away from their face. Signals don't always mean what someone might think they mean.

It is wise to keep at least 10 to 20 feet between yourself and the car in front of you while stopped. From this position, you can acccelerate and swerve into another lane or onto the shoulder in an emergency. This maneuver is even easier if you stop a little to the side, rather than in the middle, of the lane. Without this space in front of you to maneuver, you may find your escape options very limited.

In addition to the risk of being rear-ended, other emergencies for which the rider may wish to leave his lane quickly include: being approached by people on foot with hostile intentions or a sudden break down or stoppage of the car in front requiring you to merge into another lane.

STOP LIGHT CHANGING CHECKLIST

Check cross-traffic. Determine whether each driver is going to stop for, or run, the intersection;

Check for pedestrians;

Check for left-turners, whether they are signaling or not, and whether they are in the left turn lane or not;

Check the road for debris and obstructions.

PATH SELECTION 4

The Vanishing Point
As you approach a curve, the road forms a sharp point beyond which you cannot see. When entering a blind turn such as this, always ensure that you are traveling at a speed which will allow you to come to a complete stop, even while leaned over, before you reach the end of the visible roadway. You never know what lies beyond the vanishing point.

Throughout the next two chapters on path selection and braking, consider carefully how the condition and quality of your tires directly impact your safety while on the road. Swerving and turning, along with accelerating and braking, all depend on the tires for maximum performance.

SWERVING

Understanding the topic of motorcycle dynamics helps street riders cope with the many challenges faced on the public roads. One skill which requires practice is the quick swerve. Most riders are taught that the swerve is performed by counter-steering, but this is only the larger half of it. In this section, we will deconstruct the physics behind the swerve and provide a valuable alternative to the traditional swerve.

We were told when we learned to ride that when a rider pushes the left handle bar, they turn to the left. Of course, anyone who has ridden a tricycle immediately thinks this is counter-intuitive, so let's look at what is really going on. When the rider pushes the left handle bar forward (pointing the wheel to the right) the front end of the bike starts to turn to the right, just like on a tricycle. However, then something else happens.

Sir Isaac Newton tells us that a body in motion tends to stay in motion. So while the wheel makes the bikes front end turn right, the rest of the bike stays in motion going straight ahead. The rider, the frame, the rear of the bike hasn't changed direction, so the bike begins to fall to the left, which is the outside of the "tricycle turn". It is this movement of the front of the bike toward the right and the falling of the rest of the bike to the left that causes the bike to lean and begin the turn to the left. This gives us the complete picture of how a motorcycle turns. While the first part is often left out when teaching beginning street riders, understanding it opens up useful maneuvering opportunities.

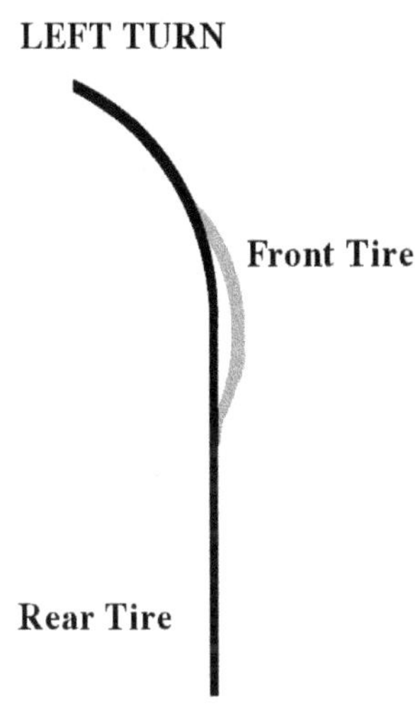

In the diagram, see how the tires begin lined up and then momentarily take different paths before rejoining. Applying this knowledge allows a change in the way obstacles are handled. First, for small obstacles already too close to swerve around in the traditional manner, riders who understand the swerve have the option of pushing left, going right, which for the purposes of this text will be called a "sidestep" as illustrated in the diagram. Of course, the result of this will be a sidestep to the right, followed by a swerve to the left. However, for a single small obstacle, the move to the right may be adequate to avoid it even when it is too close to be avoided with a typical swerve.

If given a little additional maneuvering room, a rider can induce a quick and momentary instability with a left-right combination swerve, taking advantage of a traditional swerve with the lateral space gained from the sidestep. For example, to swerve to the right around an object begin a swerve to the right with the bike's center of gravity hanging to the right (inside) of the turn. Then, at the last moment, push the left handle bar moving the bike to the other side, through the center of gravity, causing the tires to travel far to the right, providing greater space between your tires and the obstacle as described in the following exercise.

EXERCISE

The successful combination swerve requires pre-planning. The rider must learn to find the correct point in front of the obstacle at which to begin the sidestep. Starting with a turn or swerve to one side, the rider approaches the obstacle, gaining lateral distance. At the last moment before the obstacle, the rider induces a quick countersteer, causing the bike's tires to swing to the outside, farther away from the obstacle while the bike's center of gravity passes safely over the top.

From some distance away, begin approaching a cone and begin your countersteering swerve a little bit earlier than usual. At some point before passing the cone, countersteer in the opposite direction. Your bike will pass underneath you, swinging the tires out away from the obstacle. The obstacle will then pass to your side, directly underneath your body. Obviously this technique is useless for taller vertical objects such as lightpoles, but has considerable application to common low-to-the-ground obstacles such as shredded tires, potholes, roadkill, etc. With practice, you will find that this technique can be applied in a narrower lane than the traditional swerve, requiring less lateral travel, making it particularly useful in tight traffic.

DISTRACTION FIXATION

One of the biggest dangers in motorcycling comes when riders look somewhere they don't want to go. Motorcyclists call this target fixation, but of course this is a misnomer. If we were fixating on our target, we wouldn't be hurtling toward a tree. "Distraction fixation" is a more accurate term when we are focusing on something which is preventing us from safely reaching our destination.

As a rule, the more intensely someone focuses on a distraction, the less likely they are to reach their destination. Evolved from millennia of walking, our bodies naturally tend to go in whichever direction we are looking. Even when driving or riding a bike, when someone looks to the left, the vehicle will tend to wander to the left. Look right, and the vehicle will wander to the right. This effect is magnified when a rider is under stress, such as being in fear of an impending collision.

This section discusses three techniques for coping with distraction fixation. They can be used in different situations from coping with frequent minor obstacles, to high-stress split-second emergencies. The three techniques are:

1. Path Visualization
2. Pre-Loading
3. Induced Fixation

EXERCISE

Go into a parking lot and select a safe object some distance away. From a safe distance, point your motorcycle at this object and, while staring directly at it, attempt to ride away from it.

Next, select any other object and ride to it instead.

POSITIVE PATH VISUALIZATION

While language is great for conveying complex ideas, it is a very inefficient way to communicate. This is where we get the saying that a single picture is worth a thousand words. For simple concepts, such as a path of travel, a picture is easy for us to comprehend at a glance.

As is often acknowledged, the human mind can consciously keep track of about five to seven things at one time. Using path visualization allows the rider to look at a group of successive hazards and turn them into one single path. Now, instead of focusing on, say, four hazards, the rider focuses on just one path. This enables the rider to target fixate on the positive path, rather than distraction fixate on the obstacles ahead.

Path visualization is an every minute, every day, type of technique which trains the rider to look ahead, think ahead, and plan ahead. Positive Path Visualization is similar to the technique racers use when they are told to visualize their line through a turn. The difference is, on the street, there is no such thing as a static unchanging line. It must change constantly as new hazards and new information come to the rider's attention. Nevertheless, the value of the technique justifies adapting it to street riding.

To practice path visualization, first through practice and repetition, the rider develops the habit of looking far down the road. As will be discussed later in the chapter, the absolute minimum distance a rider should ever be looking at is about 400 feet, which is slightly less than a city block. As speeds increase, so too should the distance the rider looks up the road, with 800 to 1600 feet (over a quarter mile) being appropriate at higher speeds. After the rider has developed the habit of looking an adequate distance down the road, the next step is to practice maintaining an ongoing stream of intended travel through each and every obstacle that lies ahead

With practice, the rider can learn to visualize almost any path of travel, regularly creating and updating the mental map while traveling down the road. In doing so, it is possible for the rider to reduce the mental workload associated with path selection, even at critical times. Making a mental picture improves the rider's ability to cope with multiple hazards and simplifies the act of selecting the "line" or "path" down the road.

DEVELOPING POSITIVE PATH VISUALIZATION

Pick your favorite color and imagine a short, glowing, brilliant line from the front wheel of your bike going forward just a couple of feet.

Now imagine that as you look farther up the road, the line extends farther. Each time you identify an obstacle, hazard, or issue, and each time you decide whether to maneuver right or left, the line traces the path for your bike to follow.

Whether you recognize two hazards or eight, this line shows you the path to follow. And remember, this line is not unchanging. As hazards move, the line changes its course like a snake adapting to the road.

By deciding where you will go and how you will get there, you foreclose the possibility of selecting a path over the obstacles. Once you have chosen a positive path, the maneuvering becomes easier because you now have something, besides the hazards, to focus on and use as a guide.

PRE-LOADING THE BARS

Preloading the handle bars helps to circumvent the brain's natural tendency to make the body follow the eyes. This technique should be practiced under safe and controlled circumstances before being relied on in stressful or hazardous situations.

Typically, when looking off to the side of the road, such as to read a sign or make an extended glance down a side street, a rider will tend to weave a little bit in the direction that the rider is looking, usually just a few inches or a few feet. However, sometimes this tendency of the eyes to lead the body can cause dire consequences. Sufficiently distracted, it is possible to cross a center line or run onto the shoulder of a road. The best policy to avoid these situations is to always pay attention to the road ahead. However, as a practical matter, a rider's greatest safety concern isn't always directly ahead. What is needed is a way to help keep the bike traveling along its path without deviation as the rider allows attention to be focused elsewhere as needed.

When looking to the right, an experienced rider may loosen the right hand's grip on the bar or even apply a slight forward pressure to the left handle bar, as if anticipating the need to swerve to the left. While the brain's natural tendency is to try to bring the bike toward where the rider is looking, the conscious counter-pressure can balance it out and help maintain a straight line of travel down the road.

An added benefit to this technique is that, in times of stress, our muscles tend to tense up and possibly lock, leaving us with little conscious control over our direction. By preparing, with one arm already pressing forward, a startled

EXERCISE

Find a straight line and practice riding along it until you've found a speed at which you can comfortably maintain your wheels on the line. Remember that selecting a target farther down the line will assist you in staying straight, as opposed to focusing on your front wheel.

Once you are comfortable following this line, begin to ride down it and then look to the right or left. Actively concentrate on something off to the side for 3-5 seconds. Then return your attention to the line and see how far you have drifted.

Remember that this lateral distance will be magnified as speeds increase. Practice longer extended looks to the side. Become comfortable maintainng your position on the line while letting your attention be focused elsewhere.

Try different hand positions and varying levels of pressure until you find the perfect position for you. Next, practice this same exercise and after you've completed your look to the side, if you have deviated from the line, immediately swerve to the opposite side. Practice "rescuing" yourself from the deviated line of travel.

reaction may tend to exaggerate this pressure, tending to force the bike back to the proper path.

With practice, riders may extend the amount of time they can focus elsewhere without significant deviation in lane position. This technique, however, requires practice in a safe environment. Do not forget that neither oncoming cars, nor ditches on the other side are forgiving of mistakes. This is not a substitute for paying attention, but a technique for correcting a natural tendency.

SCANNING FOR ESCAPE ROUTES

Approach every quick stop with the assumption that the stopping force will not be adequate. Immediately begin scanning for the escape routes and aim your motorcycle towards one. Seldom is the back of a car the ideal object to collide with. Likely, you will prefer something just off to one side or the other of the obstacle. It may still be a straight line emergency braking maneuver, or perhaps you can spot a driveway or sidestreet that provides ample run off room for a combined brake/swerve.

Typically, the targets within your line of sight at that time will be 15-50 feet ahead of the obstacle and off to the side. Aiming for this target alone provides an extra 15-50 feet of braking distance. However, once you've achieved maximum braking, it is also likely that the experienced rider will reach a slow speed at which time it may be possible to "unlock" from the target fixation and continue onward in the other lane or on the shoulder of the road for some distance to regain position in the flow of normal traffic. But, at a minimum, the rider has gained very valuable additional stopping distance.

DELIBERATELY-INDUCED TARGET FIXATION

Distraction fixation is an easy mistake to make. While it is often thought of as a beginner mistake, even highly experienced riders can fall victim to distraction fixation because it is most likely to occur during moments of high stress. Fortunately, a cure for obstacle fixation can be implemented with a little bit of practice.

Deliberately-induced target fixation is like positive visualization with one key difference– the rider is in substantial peril which necessitates a single point of focus. When a hazard is identified far enough up the road, the path visualization technique discussed previously keeps the rider able to adapt to changing conditions, but under the most dire of circumstances, deliberately-induced target fixation can help resist the urge to fixate on the distraction. What makes the technique valuable as a last-ditch maneuver is that it harnesses the dangers of obstacle fixation and turns them into a positive force.

The first step in inducing positive target fixation is to select the best escape route. The key is to select a realistic target. Normally in emergency situations, radical movements are not options, so rather than attempt a complete change in direction, it is often better to attempt a narrow escape, seeking to just barely avoid the obstacle. Any more radical of a move adds unnecessary technical challenge to the maneuver. Looking just off to the sides of the obstacle, the rider can identify a target which is preferable to the obstacle either because it is farther down the road, or because it is more likely to provide a safe crash.

Once the route is selected, the next step is to target fixate. By forcing attention away from the distraction and creating a positive target for fixation, the rider substantially increases the odds of avoiding the obstacle.

EXERCISE

If you haven't done it ahead of time, the moment you've made the decision to emergency brake is also the moment to decide in which direction to point your motorcycle.

In this example, the car in front is stationary or coming to a rapid stop. The rider, with limited time to react must brake hard to avoid colliding with the car and, if a successful stop appears unlikely, must attempt a slight change of direction in order to gain additional stopping space. The cone to the left in this example, might be a reasonable target at which the rider can aim in such an emergency, or perhaps somewhere between the cone and the car.

When done right, the rider should narrowly miss the car and manage to come to a stop alongside the cone, or shortly past it, using the several extra feet of stopping distance.

BRAKING 5

Have you ever stopped to think about all the different types of things we have to look out for on the road?

Oil
Ice
Mud
Sand
Litter
Gravel
Leaves
Puddles
Pot holes
Road salt
Tar snakes
Metal grates
Painted lines
Shredded tires
Crowned/uneven pavement
Deep cracks in the pavement

The proper following distance between a rider and the car in front is said to be two seconds. Conservatively, this works out to be about three feet per mph. While riders are frequently reminded to maintain this following distance while underway, little is mentioned about how this cushion should be used. There is a common misconception that this space is meant to cover up for a moment's inattention or poor reaction time. However, this is incorrect. It would be absurd to recommend a "safe following distance" for riders who are not paying attention or whose reflexes are below par. If a rider's attention span or reflexes are so far outside of the norm, rule of thumb of any type would be completely inapplicable for that particular rider.

If a rider is concerned with their ability to focus and pay attention and yet must ride, backing much farther off– doubling or tripling the following distance may be a good idea. For most riders, the concept of keeping a two second (or three feet per mph) following distance has nothing to do with bad reflexes or inattention. The three feet per mph, or the two second gap, is for attentive riders with average reflexes who are focusing 100% on the task at hand, including checking mirrors, watching their speed and paying attention to traffic in all directions. Any other distractions or impediments must be accounted for additionally. Experienced riders understand that the use of a following distance strategy is far more complex than just making up for poor reaction times.

A Good Following Distance: Three Feet Per MPH

(that's one yard per mph)

Adjusting Your Gaze For Your Speed

As speeds change, so too must riding strategies. For example, at low speeds, emergency braking for a stationary obstacle offers much better chances to prevent slight incident such as a dropped bike although when traveling along the highway, swerving may provide a better opportunity to prevent a catastrophic fall and slide across the pavement. It's plain to see that an obstacle at 15mph is often going to be handled differently than when traveling at 60mph.

Just as riders must change the way obstacles will be handled at different speeds, they must also change the way they perceive those obstacles. Obeying the speed limit on the highway, a motorcycle travels at about 90 feet per second. When alert and attentive, a person's reaction time may be only a fraction of a second, but during a complex event such as riding, with the need to not only identify a hazard, but also determine a course of action before reacting, the typical reaction time is closer to 1.5 seconds. This means a motorcycle will travel about 145 feet in the time it takes the rider perceive and react to any situation. But, of course, avoiding a hazard isn't just a matter of the rider reacting, it's also a matter of the vehicle reacting– suspensions adjusting, tires flexing, and the full mass of the vehicle changing direction. Switching lanes, for example, while traveling at a brisk pace will take nearly a full second for most riders. That's another 90 feet in addition to the 145 feet it takes to react, for a total of 235 feet. Therefore, when traveling at the speed limit on the expressway, there is practically no value whatsoever to looking less than 250 feet up the road. Almost anything that is identified at 250 feet or less up the road is already in a rider's hazard zone, it is already becoming too late to react.

If a rider spots a stationary hazard at a distance greater than 250 feet up the road, there is a reasonable chance of avoiding it. Any closer and the chances get slim. A common mistake drivers and riders of all ages make is failing to keep their eyes far enough down the road. 250 feet should be the absolute minimum distance for highway driving. 400-600 feet, or more, provides significantly greater safety and security.

As a rider, you may be concerned with the SUV on the right, but whether he swerves or slams on his brakes is, in large part, dependent upon the traffic ahead of him. Your peripheral vision won't fail you as you turn your attention farther up the road.

EMERGENCY STOPS

Most emergencies give riders substantially more room to stop than they really need, but an "emergency stop" for purposes of this section is a stop which requires nearly perfect braking technique with little or no room for error. There are four possible outcomes to such an emergency stop, as presented on the following page. Examining these four possibilities can tell us everything we need to know about stopping strategies.

When in a true emergency braking situation, the goal is mitigation of risk– the risk of a collision must be counter-balanced by the risk of the rider going down from over-braking. Of the listed outcomes on the following page, number 1 is obviously the best– a safe and controlled stop. Fortunately, it is also by far the most common. Considering each of the three remaining options leads us to clear conclusions about the best way to stop and these conclusions can be summed up as the Three Principles of Street Braking.

EMERGENCY BRAKING

Four Possible Outcomes:

1. The rider can come to a successful safe stop.

2. The rider can over-apply the front brake, causing the rider to have to re-apply the front brake, losing crucial distance during an emergency stop and possibly crashing due to a locked front wheel.

3. The rider can over-apply the rear brake, causing a lock up, and lose a fraction of the 20% of braking force supplied by the rear tire for the duration of the stop, resulting in either a collision or else necessitating more aggressive front braking to compensate.

4. Underbraking. The rider can maintain a rate of braking which is nearly certain will not lock up the wheels, but may result in a low speed collision due to inadequate braking force being applied.

FIRST PRINCIPLE OF STREET BRAKING: If Something Bad is About to Happen, Make it Happen at the Slowest Speed Possible

Of the four outcomes listed, outcome number 4 (underbraking) is the second best outcome. What makes under-braking such a good outcome?

Tires are designed to provide traction against pavement. A tumbling human or a sliding steel motorcycle frame slides a lot farther and faster than a braking motorcycle tire. Simply put, if you can't stop with your tires and brakes, there's no way to stop at all. By keeping the rubber on the road and continuously applying the brakes, the bike will be at the lowest possible speed before the collision. In addition to being at the lowest possible speed, the rider has the added advantage of maintaining control of the bike until the last moment, allowing for last second maneuvering or a heavy-handed last-ditch effort at applying the brakes.

SECOND PRINCIPLE OF STREET BRAKING: The Front Brake Is the Key to Safe and Fast Stops

With the rear brake in regular habitual use, the only thing left for the rider to focus on is the front brake. The front brake can account for as much as 80% of a motorcycle's braking force. Therefore it makes sense for the rider to focus directly on the front brake during a typical emergency stop.

Braking force on a tire is dependent upon the weight applied to the tire. The more the suspension compresses, the more the bike pitches forward, and the more force can be applied to the front brake. Therefore, a steady, gradual application of the front brake helps compress the suspension farther, pitching more weight forward, allowing the front brake to become more effective and handle more load. As the front suspension pitches more weight forward, the rider is able to apply the front brake progressively harder up until the point that the tires begin to lose traction and skid.

Experienced riders describe a "chatter" coming from the front wheel before a skid occurs. The sensation is caused by the tire starting to spin more slowly than the road beneath it. If the tire comes to a stop and the road is still passing beneath it, the rider is said to be locked up and a crash is imminent. Therefore, when the chattering occurs, the rider must ease off the pressure on the front brake, not necessarily completely releasing the front brake, but rather easing off a little bit allowing the tire to catch up to the road.

THIRD PRINCIPLE OF STREET BRAKING: Always Use the Rear Brake

There are three reasons to get into the habit of using the rear brake for every stop:

IMPORTANT THINGS TO KNOW ABOUT BRAKE FLUID

Each time we apply the brakes on our motorcycle, the brakes heat up and some of this heat is transferred to the brake fluid. As the fluid gets older, it tends to absorb moisture, reducing the boiling point of the fluid. If not replaced at regular intervals, the rider will eventually encounter a time, probably while braking hard, when the brakes heat the fluid beyond its boiling point, causing tiny gas bubbles to be released into the brake line. Those tiny bubbles cause the brakes to become spongy and feel as though the brakes have gone completely out. Once the brake fluid cools however, your brakes will seem fine. Rather than take a gamble, replace your brake fluid at the manufacturer's recommended intervals.

1. A locked rear wheel still provides more braking force than a free-spinning rear wheel. Even if the rider makes a mistake and locks the tire up, it will still provide more braking force than letting the tire spin freely;

2. If the rider makes a mistake and brakes too hard causing the wheel to lock up, the rear wheel lock up is relatively simple to recover from– just keep the wheel locked until stopped to avoid the risk of a high-side crash;

3. Using the rear brake is independent of what the right hand is doing, so once braking is begun with the rear, the rider is free to focus attention on the front brake which provides the majority of the bike's braking force.

Riders need not maximize the rear tire's braking force, just so long as the brake is squeezing some braking force out of the tire. The purpose of always using the rear brake is just to pick up some additional deceleration because it's there, it's available, and using it a little bit is always better than not using it at all.

So to make best use of the rear brake, be aware that, as a motorcycle pitches forward during a stop, the rear brake becomes more prone to locking up due to less weight on the rear. The proper use of the rear brake is a somewhat hard initial application and a gradually softer application as the bike pitches forward. For this reason, riders should also keep their weight back on the bike during braking, rather than letting their body be pushed over the gas tank or handlebars. By keeping weight towards the rear of the bike, the rider takes load off the front tire and adds the load to the light rear of the bike, allowing the bike to brake harder.

Professional riders testing the braking ability of a motorcycle can make multiple stops, throw out the highest and lowest result, and average the rest... half their results are worse than they publish. And they are always on good pavement

PUTTING IT ALL TOGETHER

Here's a visualization exercise. Let's say you are traveling at 60mph on a crowded road and due to traffic conditions, you decide to maintain a safe 180 foot cushion between yourself and the car in front of you. Suddenly, the car gets on the brakes just a split second after you have turned your head to check something off to the side. By the time you turn your attention back, the driver has engaged ABS and surprises you with the fact the car's grippy tires are bringing the car to a pavement-punishing stop. The driver is on a pace to come to a complete stop within 100 feet. With your space cushion, you have a total of 280 feet to react and come to a stop and your routine glance to the side, plus the time it took you to react, cost you one second. You've now got 190 feet left to work with.

Professional riders testing the braking ability of a motorcycle can make multiple stops from 60mph, and then throw out the highest and lowest result and average the rest. On average, they can often stop in around 120-140 feet, but whatever their average is, half of their results are worse than that. Don't rely on magazine specifications to tell you how fast you can stop, because half of their results are worse than what they publish. And they are always on good pavement. So now, with 190 feet to work with on relatively unknown pavement, without having touched the brakes yet, how confident are you feeling?

Immediately, you roll off the throttle while simultaneously applying the rear brake. You begin to look to the side, checking for a better target to fixate on. Staying behind this braking car may not be your best option. You begin to also squeeze lightly on the front brake. The deceleration from the throttle roll-off, light front braking, and the rear braking cause the suspension to pitch forward- you react by pushing back with your hands or squeezing the gas tank with your knees to keep your weight balanced or slightly to the rear of the bike.

At this point, you notice that you are still gaining on the car ahead. If you maintain this amount of braking, you will clearly rear-end the driver. It may be disconcerting to realize you're gaining ground, but it simply takes longer to achieve maximum braking force on a motorcycle than it does in a car.

Since distraction fixating on the car offers little benefit, you begin looking for an escape route, trying to find something better to aim towards. You glance toward the centerline of the road and between the lanes, considering them as possible escape routes in the short moments as the suspension settles down for braking

You begin to squeeze progressively harder on the front brake, letting the suspension compress more as you squeeze. The compressing suspension pitches you a little more forward, allowing you to apply the front brakes harder. You are now near the maximum braking force and now is the time to turn your attention to the space between you and the car in front of you- is the space getting smaller? Staying the same? Or are you adding distance between the car and yourself?

If you are stopping faster than the car in front of you, then congratulations- barring any increase in his stopping rate, slickness, or debris in the road, you will come to a stop in time, but you still aren't out of danger. Check your mirrors! Is someone behind you? Are they paying attention? If the car behind you is catching up, be prepared to either swerve into another lane or else trade away your

space cushion. You might have to accept the risk of possibly rear-ending the car in front to give the driver behind you more space if it looks like he's going to need it.

But what if you are braking as hard as you are comfortable with and still gaining on the car in front of you? If so, your following distance has failed you. You likely won't have time to worry about what's behind you. It's time to make a decision: are you more confident that the traction will hold if you brake harder? Or are you more willing to accept a low speed crash? Either way, it's time to use up that space cushion.

If you are an inexperienced rider or have never experienced chatter on the front wheel, you might try and bet that there is at least a little bit more braking force available than you have used before. You will squeeze harder on the brake lever while remaining prepared for that "chatter" on the front wheel that tells you that you are braking too hard for the tires. Approaching the car in front, remember that every fraction of a second you remain on two wheels will substantially reduce the speed of your collision. You'd better hope you can find an escape route.

If you can imagine the above scenario, and if it concerns you, ask yourself again about your space cushion. What is adequate? What is safe for you?

Though high-performance braking on the street increases the risk of going down during the exercise, experimentation under somewhat controlled conditions may prevent more severe mistakes when hard braking is absolutely critical to the rider's survival

PRACTICE BRAKING

The process of braking on the street is more involved than just the mechanical and physical attributes of the motorcycle. It also consists of properly applied experience that can greatly enhance the rider's braking results. When a rider finds adequate stopping distance and space to practice, there are two valuable maneuvers that can be performed to help riders prepare for an emergency.

Though high-performance braking on the street increases the risk of going down during the exercise, experimentation under somewhat controlled conditions may prevent more severe mistakes when hard braking is critical to the rider's survival. Knowledge gained from these exercises can be used as information in adjusting the rider's following distances and also in determining how much force will be available during a swerve or emergency turn. These exercises are trade-offs in which safety is lessened under safer circumstances in exchange for greater experience to be used under potentially more dangerous situations in the near future. It is, needless to say, a trade-off which all riders should consider carefully for themselves as it comes with its own set of risks.

HARD BRAKING THE REAR WHEEL

Whenever going out for a ride, it may be prudent for the rider to begin with a couple of rear-only braking exercises on the way down the street. This allows the rider to get a feel for how much traction is available on the road at a given place and time. The rider need not completely lock up the rear brake; only apply what is deemed to be an acceptable amount of force to see whether the tires can maintain the expected level of braking force under the present road conditions. By making a habit of being aggressive with rear-wheel braking exercises in low speed non-emergency situations, a rider can regularly keep track of how much traction is available. (Cautionary note: Using more rear brake than is necessary for safe and controlled travel may result in a crash, possibly a high-side crash. Don't do it if you are not comfortable with the potential dangers).

PRACTICE PROGRESSIVE BRAKING

The goal of a progressive braking exercise is to minimize the risk of a high speed front wheel lock up during an emergency by acclimatizing the rider to the bike's braking ability and characteristics under safer conditions.

From a modest speed, begin by rolling off the throttle as you apply the rear brake. Then as the bike's suspension begins to settle, begin with a gentle application of the front brake and slowly increase the amount of braking force as the suspension compresses, ideally bringing the front tire to near-lockup as the speedometer reaches zero. This practice takes not only the available traction into consideration, but also the motorcycle as a whole, including the suspension and even the rider's weight-shifting habits. By starting with a conservative estimate of traction during the first stop and slowly applying greater stopping force as the bike slows down, riders can get a better feel for how much following distance is needed for current conditions while ensuring that any lock up that may occur will happen at a very low speed, thereby reducing the risk in this high performance braking exercise below the risk that would be faced in a true emergency stop. This also helps riders assess their own braking habits to ensure they are in peak form when the need arises. (Cautionary note: Using excessive braking can cause a crash. Don't do it on this author's recommendation unless you are willing to risk a crash.)

In addition to practicing these techniques on the way down the street, each unpopulated stop sign without traffic or other dangers (including no traffic to your rear) provides the rider with another opportunity to examine the adequacy of the braking force provided under present conditions. However, always bear in mind that intersections, where traffic frequently stops, often tends to have greater amounts of oil and other debris on the roadway, making intersections a somewhat hazardous place to practice braking.

STRATEGIES FOR BRAKING ON LOW TRACTION SURFACES

Every day, cars with leaking fluids such as oil and antifreeze deposit small drops onto the pavement which sink down into the cracks and crevices. When rain fills these cracks and crevices, the oil and other junk rises to the surface and creates a large oil slick. When there is heavy morning dew, a light rain, or in the first minutes of a heavy rain, the risk of oil on the road is greatest. Many riders recommend stopping for the first 30 to 60 minutes of a rain storm to give the oil an opportunity to clear the roadway. The longer it has been between rain showers, the more prudent this advice may be.

There are some other surfaces that provide poor or unknown braking qualities. Some of the worst surfaces are stripes, arrows, other painted markings, manhole covers, the rubber sound-

Bad weather. Standing water, possibly lots of oil and other slick stuff on the road. Even the visibility is bad. These are the times to think twice about whether your space cushion is really as safe as you think. This is the time to use a strategy for low traction braking.

dampeners used on railroad track crossings, grated bridge crossings, and metal plates that are frequently used to cover up large holes in the street. All of these surfaces are likely to provide virtually no traction to the rider. To cope with these obstacles, keep the bike upright and cruise through at a perpendicular angle to the obstruction without any unnecessary accelerating or braking.

Sometimes it is necessary to brake over slippery surfaces. In these cases, it is advisable to greatly reduce the amount of pressure applied to the front brake and rely on the rear brake to the greatest extent possible. Also, an abrupt shift, a quick stab on the brakes, or a jerky turn upsets the suspension and can cause a loss of traction in an otherwise manageable situation. Therefore, the rider should always match RPMs when shifting, avoid "dumping" the clutch, squeeze the brake lever progressively, and make all turns smooth and fluid to avoid upsetting the suspension when the going gets slippery.

SQUEEZING THE BRAKES

There is some debate over the appropriate way to squeeze the front brake. Some schools advocate the rider using the entire hand on the throttle, and then transition to four fingers on the brake when necessary. Other schools train riders to use two fingers on the brakes. This topic is hotly debated with most street-riding schools deciding to train all riders to use four fingers while most track/racing schools teach the rider to use two fingers. Neither approach is wrong, however there is certainly a 'correct' approach for each rider and it depends on a number of factors.

The logic behind four-fingered braking is twofold. First, it ensures the rider will have enough strength to fully apply the front brake. Secondly, it has been found that even experienced riders, when panicked, will tend to reach for the brake with all four fingers. Therefore, by practicing the use of four fingers, the rider will be assured of having trained muscle-memory to achieve a successful emergency stop when grabbing unconsciously with all four fingers.

The counterpoint to the four-fingered braking is that, first, two-fingered braking allows riders to cover the brake while still accelerating. Second, nearly all bikes nowadays have sufficiently powerful brakes that a full lock-up is achievable with only two fingers. And third, you can train your muscles to brake with two fingers just as with four.

While both positions have merit, there is ample research indicating that riders who use two fingers will be in jeopardy of grabbing with four fingers in a panic. However, there is the common sense issue that you cannot easily maintain throttle position while covering the brake if you are using four fingers. This means the rider who brakes with four fingers will be less likely to cover the brake until it has been determined that rolling off the throttle is appropriate. Therefore the rider who brakes with two fingers can cover the brakes earlier than the rider using four fingers.

Because of the risk that a rider using two-fingered braking will revert to four fingers at the worst possible time, for any rider considering two finger braking, a further step is appropriate to combat this natural tendency. The rider must get out of the habit of using five fingers on the throttle. Keeping the index and middle fingers loose and open even when not covering the brake will encourage the rider to cover the brake more frequently and to use these two fingers in a panic situation.

As a result of the above considerations, the following checklist can be used in assessing which approach is better for a particular rider.

FOUR VS TWO FINGER BRAKING

If you answer yes to each of the following questions, then two fingered braking is likely to be an appropriate choice for use on the street.

Are you physically comfortable covering the brake for 15 or 20 minutes non-stop while riding?

Are you in the habit of going for a ride and never, even once, using 5 fingers on the throttle (they may rest on the throttle, but are not actually squeezing it)?

Do you often find yourself in situations where you are simultaneously accelerating while also anticipating the need to brake?

TWO FINGER BRAKING

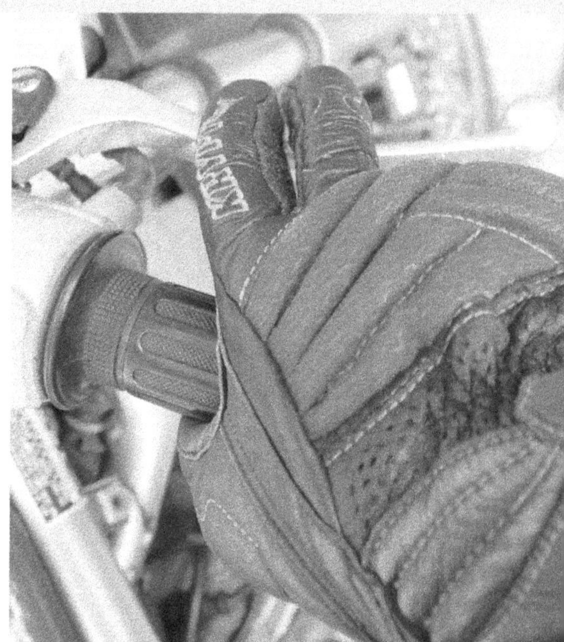

With the two finger approach, the transition from twisting the throttle to front-wheel braking can be accomplished seamlessly. Also, using the brake and throttle together for brief periods is a common technique under limited high performance scenarios.

Using the two finger approach, it is possible to "cover" the front brake, getting ready for a fast stop, even before you've decided to slow down. This is particularly valuable in dynamic situations where brisk acceleration may offer the best escape route, but a precious second or two will disappear before the right course of action becomes clear. Accidents occurring immediately in front of the rider and some complicated intersections often fall into this category. This technique is also helpful when approaching curves, allowing the rider to match engine RPM' while downshifting, even as the rider slows down for the turn. The ability to downshift smoothly while braking keeps the rider in the right gear for their speed, assisting them in being ready to accelerate quickly after completing the braking maneuver.

If you choose to use two finger braking, it is best to get out of the habit of five finger accelerating. You should never need five fingers on the throttle and by keeping your index and middle finger loose on the throttle, it will encourage you to reach for the brake with those two fingers in an emergency situation. Ultimately, it's all about what is comfortable for you and the way you ride.

The Two Second Rule, by Distance

Many schools recommend a 2 second following distance between your vehicle and the one in front. You can also calculate out the distances. Mathematically, these two approaches are nearly identical, so if you prefer 2 seconds, use it. Personally, I find it easier to estimate distance than time and I think that counting to two gets boring quickly. If you are comfortable estimating distances, then here are some "ballpark figures" you can use to judge safe distances for given speeds. They aren't perfect, but are all accurate to within 10%

15mph = 45 feet = wheelbase of a typical semi trailer
20mph = 60 feet = foul line to the first pin on a regulation bowling alley; or pitcher's rubber to homeplate in major league baseball
30mph = 90 feet = home to first base
45mph = 135 feet = catcher to second base
60mph = 180 feet = midfield to the goalpost of a football field

RIDING PHYSIOLOGY 6

PERCEPTION

It is difficult for a rider to accurately assess the speed and acceleration of an oncoming car and it is even more difficult for drivers to assess the speed of a motorcycle. In the day, riders can use the size of a car in their vision to judge its distance. At night, riders can look at two headlights and estimate the rate at which they are becoming larger and farther apart; this provides a hint as to how quickly the car is approaching. However, drivers don't have the same abilities with motorcycles.

Motorcycles are less common and drivers simply don't have as much experience judging the speed or closure rate of a motorcycle. Secondly, motorcycles are smaller, thus making it more difficult to perceive the change in size which we are accustomed to using to judge speed. Thirdly, motorcycles only have a single headlight (or if they have two, they are spaced very closely together which may make them appear at night to be a single car very far off in the distance).

Motorcyclists are dependent upon their body to a much greater degree than drivers. While riding a motorcycle, a rider's body may be forced to endure substantial stresses. Eyesight may be strained by a greater amount of light entering the eyes than is experienced in an enclosed car. Hearing is always reduced on a motorcycle, whether by wind noise or ear plugs. The vibrations of the motorcycle and the potentially punishing effects of the wind can tire the rider's body quickly. Drugs, alcohol, and mental distractions are also more hazardous on a motorcycle due to the increased risks faced while riding. All combined, it is easy to see why riders must be diligent in assessing the dangers and risks imposed upon their bodies by both external as well as internal factors.

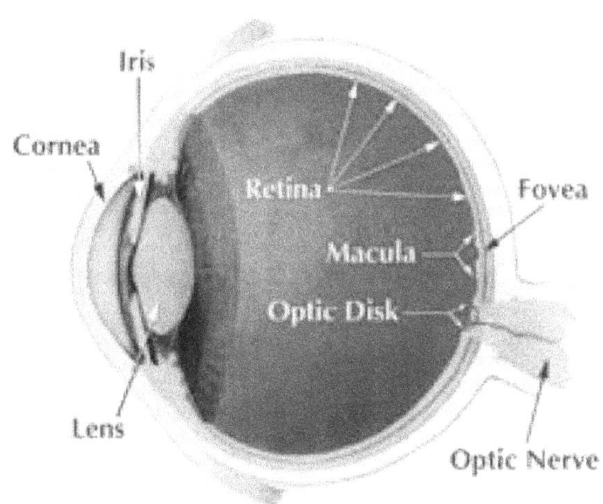

Diagram of the human eye. The retina holds photo-receptive cells that allow us to see the outside world. These cells transmit their signals to the optic disk, which is responsible for passing the visual data to the brain via the optic nerve. The optic disk contains no photo-receptive cells and this is the cause of the human blindspot.

RIDING VISION

Anyone who has looked all over for their keys only to find them in the first place they looked understands how it is possible to "look" and yet not "see". This everyday occurrence may be attributable to the human blind spot.

Light from the outside world passes through the front of our eye and hits the retina, which is comprised of photo-sensitive cells and creates small electrical impulses that are passed along via the optic nerve to the brain for processing. The blind spot is located at the optic disk where there is a hole for the optic nerve to pass through from the eye into the brain. This hole, with its lack of photoreceptors is the cause of the human blind spot.

The blind spot is not normally a problem because our two eyes work together. The arrangement makes it nearly impossible for an object to be in both blind spots at once for any extended length of time. However, when one eye is temporarily blocked, whether by a pillar in the car, or a light pole, or any other obstruction, it is easy for an object in plain sight to "disappear". Of course, if the rider already knows an object is there, the brain simply does not accept the disappearance and so it responds with a double-take or a closer look, moving the eyes around until the object reappears. This happens almost instantaneously and for this reason people are seldom aware of the natural blind spot in their vision.

Always Look With Both Eyes!

Whenever looking for traffic, pedestrians or other hazards, use both eyes in each direction and give them the necessary time to focus; this can take as long as a full second (count to one one-thousand). Using just one eye, or failing to give the eyes time to focus will allow details to go unnoticed, leaving some part of the picture hidden in the blind spot. This can makes a quick one-eyed glance as bad as not looking at all.

To ensure both eyes are actively working together, look around obstacles such as the light posts or a car alongside you. The rider must move around on the seat, peek around corners with both eyes, lean forward and back, and do whatever is necessary to look actively with both eyes. One strategy riders can use to ensure they are using both eyes is to look with their nose, meaning to point the nose directly in the direction they wish to look. Being in the center, using the nose ensures that both eyes will have a clear view in whatever direction the rider looks.

Close your left eye and bring your face close to the page. Keeping your head facing forward, look over toward the + sign with your right eye. Now slowly pull the book away from your face. At some point, the motorcycle will disappear. This is the blind spot in our vision. Everyone has it. The best thing we can do is be aware of it.

Keep in mind when approaching an intersection that it is likely that a driver decelerating toward an intersection at the same rate may not know to use both eyes. It is therefore possible that a motorcycle can actually remain hidden behind the car's pillar for an extended period of time and blocked from the driver's other eye by the blind spot as the rider slows down.

The Night Blind Spot

The human eye uses two different types of receptors to view or recognize an object. The first type is the cone-shaped receptor which provides a sharp, clear, color image to our brain. When we try to focus in on an object, it is these cone-shaped receptors that provide us with the sharp, detailed image. The reason we "focus in" on an object to view it in detail is that the cones are highly-concentrated around the center of the retina, in the area known as the fovea.

The second type of receptors are rod-shaped. They are concentrated around the periphery, surrounding the cones, and make up your peripheral vision. Rods do not perceive color and do not have the sharpness of focus: they lack acuity. However, they are almost 1,000 times more sensitive to light and perceive motion more quickly, which is the reason people often "catch something out of the corner of their eye."

Working together, the cones and rods allow the human eye to be more perceptive to movement around the periphery of our vision and then when we move our eyes toward that object, we can get a clearer, more colorful, and more detailed view.

During the daytime, we use the center of our vision, known as the foveal cone, to focus in on objects and see them with the most clarity. However, at night this method of viewing does not work as well. Under darkening conditions, colors become more difficult to see. When darkness begins to set in, it first becomes difficult to distinguish blues from blacks. When it gets darker, dark reds may become difficult to differentiate as well. Eventually, all colors become less perceptible and the world takes on a more monotone appearance.

Monochromatic rods needed for low light vision take considerably longer– sometimes an hour or more– to fully adapt

As our ability to perceive color deteriorates, a blind spot begins to develop in the center of our vision due to the absence of rod receptors in this area. The foveal cone, the one degree of sharpest vision in the human eye filled almost exclusively with cone receptors becomes almost useless, unable to perceive things as lighting gets reduced. This means that under dark conditions, beyond street lights and well-traveled roads, the absence of rods in the fovea causes objects a rider stares at to appear to fade away and then gradually become more visible as they move toward the periphery of the rider's vision. This is referred to as the "Night Blind Spot" and it is as large as a 5 to 10 degree cone extending from our eyes.

Our brains adjust for much, though not all, of our eyes' shortcomings. We are unlikely to notice our inability to see straight ahead unless an object far ahead suddenly disappears in front of our eyes. To combat this, riders must use their peripheral vision and rely more on what can be seen from the edges of their vision. Under these conditions, "zoning out" or staring blankly ahead at the road can be especially hazardous. While a bright brake light may be plainly visible by the color-sensing cones, a more distant, less bright light may go unseen and less conspicuous dangers, such as a tire in the road, or an

An approximation of the amount of visual information lost to the rider under darkening conditions.

animal may be impossible to notice. In order to ensure that the rider's peripheral vision gets a chance to see down the road, it is critical to maintain a scan of at least 15 to 20 degrees going from side to side or up and down, such that the middle of the road is regularly viewed not just from the center, but also from the corners of the eyes.

Adapting to Night Vision

Eyes take time to adjust to darkness. Rods and cones perceive light through the use of photopigments which send electrical signals to the brain when exposed to light, but require darkness to regenerate. Color-sensing cones exposed to bright light will regenerate in 5 to10 minutes, however, the monochromatic rods needed for low light vision take considerably longer- sometimes an hour or longer- to fully adapt. There are four things riders can do to improve their ability to see at night.

First, allow time for the eyes to adapt. It can take up to 10 minutes for the human eye to obtain a reasonable amount of night vision and this ability will then continue to improve over the course of an hour or more. As a result, anything which can be done to protect the eyes from bright lights will be beneficial. At night, some pilots opt to wear sunglasses when making brief stops at an airport. In an effort to retain night vision on dark roads, some riders will close one eye as an approaching vehicle comes near. By doing this, they preserve more of their night vision in one of their eyes. Other riders find this to be too distracting.

Second, riders can reduce the level of light on their vehicle. Instrument lights, map lights, reading lights, and navigation systems all allow light into the rider's eyes, either directly or by reflection. Each of these lights reduces the rider's ability to see in the dark. In addition, this is made worse when the light reflects off of windshield and into the rider's eye. As a result, all lights on the bike should be kept to a minimum comfortable level to maintain night adapted vision.

Third, consume adequate amounts of vitamin A. Vitamin A is converted to retinol within the human body and is used by the photoreceptors to replenish the photopigments. The greatest sources of Vitamin A are meat and dairy products such as milk, butter, cheese, and eggs. It is also found in carrots, spinach, broccoli leaves, sweet potatoes, pumpkin, and cantaloupe.

Fourth, avoid sources of carbon monoxide. Carbon monoxide has a negative effect on night vision and adaptability. As a result, one should avoid inhaling exhaust fumes or smoking cigarettes before riding at night.

Many people believe that night-adapted eyes are less affected by red light. There is some truth to this in certain circumstances, however even red light will significantly reduce your night-adapted vision. In general, the best policy is to keep all visible lights to a minimum.

DEVELOPING A SCAN

Important information arises constantly all around us. While riding, it is crucial to plan a strategy which ensures the rider will perceive this information as quickly as possible. One good habit is to develop a series of active riding scans. By repeatedly checking the same items in the same order, the rider develops a routine that works consistently, preventing the risk of overlooking crucial details.

The advantage of the scan lies in its repeatability and consistency. By forming habits around the way you scan for information, the chance of missing something crucial is reduced. The scan should adjust based upon variables the rider encounters, or expects to encounter, at particular times. For instance, a rider might develop a particular scan for waiting on a green light at intersections and a different scan for when approaching the intersection with the right of way. At night, it is imperative to make a wider scan in order to make better use of our eyes' peripheral vision. On highways, the rider may find it necessary to pay a little extra attention to the speedometer.

While most of a rider's attention should be focused on the road ahead, the occasional and consistent check of mirrors and gauges will protect the rider from surprises. What follows is a good general purpose scan.

1. Road directly ahead
2. Road off to left and right sides
(also allowing your eyes a peripheral view of the road ahead)
3. Gauges
4. Road ahead and to the sides again
5. Mirrors

HEARING

Motorcycling tends to present a challenging environment for ears. The motorcycles themselves tend to be rather loud, especially if fitted with an aftermarket exhaust. However, when a rider gets up to about 40 mph, the wind noise generally makes up a greater proportion of the total sound heard by the rider. In this environment, riders must keep their ears attuned to sirens and other auditory indications of hazards on the roadway.

The sound we perceive in our ears comes from sound waves which travel through the air in pulses of alternating high and low pressures which form a soundwave. The stronger the pressure change in the wave, the louder the sound. The loudness of a sound is measured in decibels (dBA) and fortunately for riders, the Occupation Safety and Health Administration (OSHA) has done considerable research on the effects of high sound pressure levels on the human ear and much of the information should be heeded by riders.

PERMISSIBLE NOISE EXPOSURES
Maximum Sound Level Duration Per Day

Hours	*dBA*
8 hours	*90*
6 hours	*92*
4 hours	*95*
3 hours	*97*
2 hours	*100*
90 minutes	*102*
60 minutes	*105*
30 minutes	*110*
15 minutes	*115*

Generally, continued exposure to sound levels of 80 decibels or higher will cause long term hearing damage and unfortunately, this is also about as quiet as a motorcycling can possibly get without the assistance of ear plugs. Some signs that a rider has been exposed to hazardous noise levels include pain or ringing in the ear, or noticing that the speech of others sounds muffled or dull after a ride.

While the temporary sensations of hearing loss fade over time, these slight exposures to elevated sound pressures do cause slight and irreversible damage every time a rider starts up a motorcycle. This damage is gradual and seldom noticed, however the effects are cumulative over a rider's lifetime.

Noise Reduction Strategies

Because hearing loss is irreversible, it should be protected from the outset of every ride as damage can be done before the injury is noticed. Wearing a cheap set of foam ear plugs can easily reduce the amount of noise by 20 decibels or more. Fortunately, ear plugs are widely available at drug stores and there is a wide selection to choose from. If a particular ear plug feels uncomfortable or fits poorly, other brands can be tried. There is an almost unlimited number of different styles to choose from.

In addition to ear plugs, other ways to reduce the risk of hearing damage while riding include retaining stock mufflers, using an effective windshield, and a quiet helmet.

Definitive information on helmet noise is difficult to find because, to a degree, the noise inside of a helmet is dependent upon the head that is inside it and at the time of this writing, there is no extensive helmet test-ride program to assist riders in evaluating helmets. However, reviews and tests can be used to get an idea for how loud a helmet might be and some manufacturers are known to put great emphasis on ergonomics and noise reduction issues. Riders can also begin to estimate how loud it will be inside a helmet by looking for a number of factors that often increase the noise level such as poorly sealed vents that will allow air to whistle through even when closed and a poorly-sealed face shield. However, the most drastic cause of noise within a helmet comes from the bottom, where there is a large open space for the rider's head. This space can be minimized with the use of a collar that goes around the base of the helmet and blocks the wind from entering.

The loudness of a helmet is also partly dependent upon the windshield of the motorcycle. The amount of noise a rider perceives can be greatly influenced by the way the windshield interacts with a particular helmet and larger windshields are not always better. Riders would be well advised to experiment with as many different windshields or positions as possible and select those that work best for the speeds at which the rider most frequently rides. Of course, in the case of an adjustable windshield, the rider can adjust the height while underway. This can have a significant affect on quietness while riding.

THE BODY

No motor vehicle demands as much interaction between the rider and machine as a motorcycle. In addition to the controls that the rider must operate, the rider's body itself is used as a crucial tool for safe and effective motorcycle operation. Legs are used when coming to a stop and also for absorbing bumps; arms are used to keep the rider centered on the bike; the rider's entire body is shifted side-to-side to help negotiate turns. This high degree of rider interaction means that, to a greater degree than in any other vehicle, a motorcycle rider's physical well-being is a crucial factor in reducing risk.

There are a number of physical factors that impact a rider's ability to operate a motorcycle effectively. Physical limitations such as height or strength may limit a rider's choices when selecting a new bike. While it is true that an

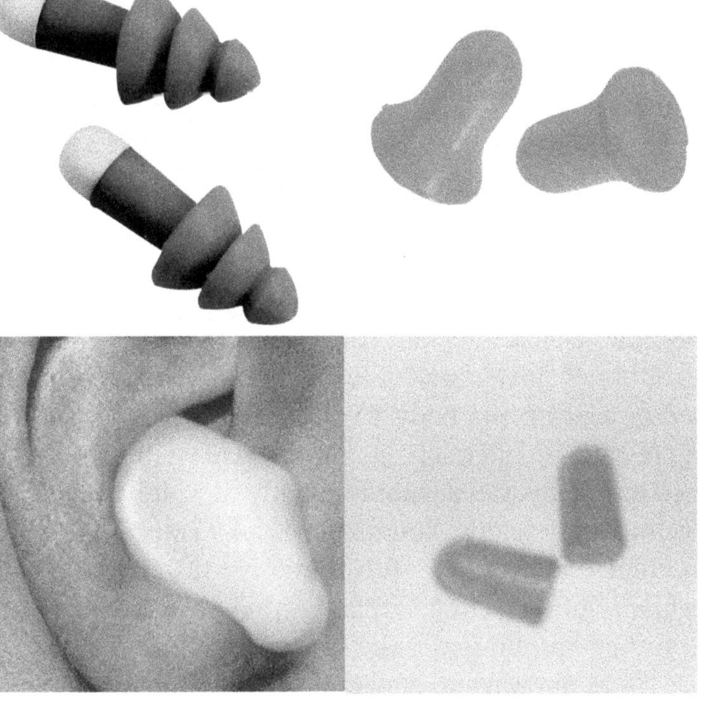

experienced rider can often handle a bike that is too tall or too heavy, it may not be comfortable and it certainly adds in an extra risk factor when riding. A rider's condition at the time of a ride also plays a part in determining how much risk the rider will face. Some of these problems are environmental, such as dehydration, hypothermia, and hyperthermia while others are self-induced such as sleepiness, medication, alcohol, mental fatigue, or distraction. Any one of these situations alone may be sufficient to cause a serious accident on the roadway. In combination, it can get much worse.

This is not a First Aid text. To find details on first aid treatment for any of the conditions below, always consult with trusted authorities on the subject.

Dehydration

On a nice sunny day, the sun beats down on the rider's skin heating it up. So the body sweats, cooling the rider by the evaporation of the sweat on the rider's skin. However, when it comes to motorcycling, there is one problem with this scenario: human bodies are not adapted for evaporative cooling with 40mph winds. As a result, the sweat evaporates faster and the skin heats up again causing the body to sweat more. As a result, a rider on a motorcycle will become dehydrated more quickly despite feeling physically comfortable. A rider becomes dehydrated substantially faster while motorcycling than while just standing around under the sun.

Some ways to stay cool while riding and reduce the risk of dehydration include wearing a jacket, which keeps the sun from beating down on the rider's skin and allows the rider to control the amount of airflow and evaporation off the skin. Also, a wet bandana, tee-shirt, or neck cooler can help reduce the amount of sweat the body must generate to keep cool.

Some symptoms of dehydration include thirst, loss of appetite, dry skin, dizziness, skin flushing, dark colored urine, dry mouth, fatigue or weakness, chills, head rushes, increased heart rate, increased respiration, decreased sweating, elevated body temperature, fatigue, muscle cramps, nausea, vomiting, headaches, and confusion.

To prevent dehydration, our bodies need water and also electrolytes (potassium and sodium). Electrolytes are found in fruits and vegetables as well as their juices. Sports drinks are also a good quick source of electrolytes.

Hyperthermia and heat stroke

When the body gets dehydrated and stops producing as much sweat, or when subjected to high temperatures, the rider faces the risks of hyperthermia and heat stroke.

Riders suffering from hyperthermia may become disoriented or confused. In addition, blood pressure may drop causing fainting or dizziness. Skin may become red as the blood vessels dilate and the rider may feel hot. After this phase, the rider may begin to experience the chills, nausea, and convulsions. Riders may even experience temporary blindness.

Hypothermia

Motorcyclists also face greater risks when the temperatures begin to drop. People living in northern climates are well acquainted with the concept of wind chill. For any given temperature, the faster the wind blows, the more quickly a rider's warmth is transferred from the skin to the air. For example, at 60ºF at 60 mph, the air feels like 41ºF. Certainly, a warm jacket and gloves would be adequate, but when the temperature drops to 40ºF, riding along at 60 mph feels like 9ºF. And as temperatures drop below freezing, anything above 30 mph will feel like negative degrees Fahrenheit.

For as cold as the temperature may feel when riding around on a chilly morning, it gets worse when the rain starts to fall. Rain can turn a cool day into a dangerously cold one by efficiently drawing warmth away from the rider's skin. This means that even on a relatively nice day, it is possible to suffer from the effects of hypothermia, which include loss of muscle coordination and difficulty thinking (consciously thinking about where the brake lever or throttle is located, or at what speed to put your foot down are pretty good clues). Other symptoms of hypothermia include drowsiness, fatigue, stumbling, amnesia, poor judgment, hallucinations, loss of perceptual contact with the environment, and dilated pupils.

Keeping Warm, Keeping Dry, Keeping Safe

When riding in colder temperatures, layered clothing will help keep the rider comfortable. The first layer should wick away moisture. This so-called "wicking layer" should be non-absorbent. It is intended to allow moisture, such as sweat, to be pulled away from the body to prevent the rider from having to feel wet and clammy during the ride. The next layer, called the mid-layer, contains insulating fabrics such as cotton or fleece, which traps warm air near the body and holds it there. In large part it is the air, not the fabric, that provides the insulation. The outer layer is wind-proof and, in the case of rain gear, water-proof. While the mid layer traps a lot of air, it would allow the wind to blow right through it, limiting its effectiveness as an outer layer. The outer layer, therefore, helps keep the air trapped in the inner layers, providing warmth.

When preparing for the rain, riders will discover that minimal rain gear, even for extended journeys, isn't too difficult to pack. A rain suit and water proof riding gloves go a long way to keeping a rider comfortable in the rain. Add in waterproof boots and a well-sealed full face helmet, and a rider should be able to stay mostly dry and comfortable across a long stretch of pavement. For shorter trips, the rain suit alone will make a big difference and it's cheap to buy and easy to carry along. Most importantly, when the temperature starts to drop, the rain coat can double as a very effective wind-blocker, allowing the rider to continue on in greater comfort even as the temperature drops.

Rain Suits

Most uninsulated rain suits can roll up and store conveniently in a pouch that the rider can stash somewhere on the motorcycle. Many riders make do with a generic "banana suit" (available through hardware stores and other work-type retailers), which typically is ridiculously baggy and bright yellow, consisting of pants and a jacket. Generally these are cheap and work well, though tend to be bulky to pack. Very thin materials are available and some hold up better than others. There are motorcycle-specific garments out there that will tend to be better at keeping horizontal rain off your body, but camping outfitters and companies catering to outdoors enthusiasts generally have something that will work.

The fact that rain suits are typically windproof makes them equally useful as windbreakers when the temperatures dip unexpectedly. A mesh jacket with a rain suit may seem to be a strange combination on a sunny day, but it can certainly help keep a rider warm. Some other considerations when selecting a rain suit include:

Color- generally a bright, highly visible color will add to your ability to be seen in bad conditions.

Reflectivity- in addition to bright color, some riders seek out suits which have some reflective material to improve visibility even farther.

Air circulation- humid conditions aren't conducive to evaporating sweat and most rain suits in warm weather tend to be sticky. However, anything that can be done to get some air flowing will generally be an improvement. Many rain jackets have zippers in the back, behind a flap, which helps keep rain out while allowing some air to blow through.

Sealing at the limbs- buttons, Velcro, or elastic at the arms and ankles help keep a rider dry and prevent the suit from "ballooning" at higher speeds.

Riding Gloves

Gore-Tex® or similar water-blocking fabric in a glove goes a long way to helping keep a rider's hands dry and comfortable. It is also possible to buy over-gloves that slide over a rider's regular gloves to make them water proof. Over-gloves tend to pack smaller, but even a normal waterproof riding glove won't take up much space beneath the seat and the extra pair is nice to have.

When wearing gloves in the rain, it's a good idea to tuck the gloves inside the jacket. This will keep the water on your arms from running down and filling the glove with water.

One feature that is available on some gloves is a small strip of rubber on the left index finger which serves as a face shield wiper. A rider should be careful, however, to ensure the face shield is free from grit before sliding the rubber squeegee across the face shield, potentially causing a gouge or scratch to the polycarbonate face shield.

Rain Boots

When riding in the rain, the feet are the toughest thing to keep dry and comfortable. Riders use their feet for braking, shifting, keeping upright at a stop. Keeping feet comfortable provides a huge increase in comfort during a wet ride.

Helmet

You likely won't know how good your helmet is in the rain until you've tried it under wet conditions. Here are some tips to help your helmet perform at its best.

Many full face helmets have an air duct that directs air onto the back of the face shield. This helps control fogging which becomes more of an issue in the rain. To reduce fogging even farther, it is possible to make a solution out of water and a small amount of dish soap. Cleaning the face shield (and glasses wearers can also clean their lenses) with this solution helps to prevent fog from forming. There are also commercially available products that work similarly.

Some helmets leak, or don't provide a seal. Three-quarter helmets often have this problem– allowing rain to sneak in on the inside of the face shield. This is significantly more difficult to remove while riding. If a rider should find vision being significantly impaired by water, it is wise to stop and take a break, rather than push on without adequate vision.

TIP FOR GLASSES WEARERS

It's a bit of a hassle to dry off your glasses while riding in the rain, so if riding with a full face helmet, be careful to put your face shield down before moving forward, or else the water will start to hit your glasses and drying glasses in the rain is often a difficult task while exposed to the elements on a motorcycle.

SELF-INDUCED RISK FACTORS

In addition to all the potential hazards faced in the normal course of riding a motorcycle, humans sometimes add their own risk factors. Riding while distracted, tired, fatigued, hung-over, intoxicated, or under the influence of drugs either prescribed or over the counter, are all factors which require riders to exercise additional care should they decide to ride at all.

Distractions can be very mind-consuming

Distractions can be very mind-consuming. While many people ride to clear their head or take a break from it all, the key point to understand is that the common strategy is to leave the troubles behind and focus on the task of riding 100%. Getting a new perspective on the same old problem or changing scenery to think about the problems in a new light is probably an endeavor best avoided while motorcycling. It is very rare while riding that the rider doesn't have some things to be focusing on pertaining to the ride. Mindless moments on the street are few and far between. So before you let your mind wander and before you allow distractions to creep in, consider the ride itself. Ask how safe it is to disengage your brain from this hazardous activity.

Riding while fatigued or tired can also have a bad result. While being tired is largely a function of sleep, fatigue can set in even while the body is completely awake. Many people with stressful jobs or who engage in mentally challenging tasks will find they are dramatically less mentally aware of their surroundings as they leave. While there is no exact way to say at what point tiredness or fatigue becomes a dangerous factor while riding, the rider should keep in mind that the effect is real and best avoided. A rider can experiment carefully with these factors and slowly and cautiously develop strategies and limits of when to ride and when the bike is best left on the sidestand.

Drugs can also have a negative effect on riders. These drugs may be prescribed or over the counter. Even alcohol and its after effects (hangovers) can cause a rider to perform poorly. Alcohol is involved in nearly half of all motorcycling accidents. A rider with any alcohol in their system is five times more likely to be involved in a crash. This statistic is indicative of a rider who is hung-over. By contrast, a rider who is actively drinking, even with a Blood Alcohol Content in the legal range, of .05% or higher is 40 times more likely to be involved in a crash.

All these factors are self-induced. In these cases, riders take the risks upon themselves and make the conscious decision to ride while impaired. Whether the impairment is caused by alcohol, fatigue, tiredness, or distractions, riders must consider the situation carefully for themselves before throwing a leg over a motorcycle.

SELF ASSESSMENT 7

The "as if we don't have enough to worry about" Category

In California, spark plugs are stolen for use as crack pipes
In Indiana, snipers have been known to shoot at motorcyclists
In Chicago, kids have dropped rocks and bricks off overpasses onto vehicles below
In Florida, alligators can be seen on the sides of some roads
In Alaska, bears get hungry right before winter and can be seen foraging for food near the roadside

Not every inch of pavement poses a hazard to the experienced rider. Most of the time, riding is a simple enough undertaking requiring little skill beyond the basics that were learned during the first few weeks of riding. However, even these moments of relative comfort can tell us a lot about our condition and readiness to continue riding. Tiny mistakes made during the easy moments of riding can indicate potential problems that may arise when a rider's skills get put to the test.

Riders do not normally swerve out of their lanes, miss stop signs, or fail to hold a steady speed. However, when a motorcyclist gets tired, distracted, or has other factors coming into play, it is easy to occasionally make a mistake. Ninety-nine out of a hundred times these mistakes are meaningless and go unseen by anyone except the rider. The temptation may be to blow it off, forget it, and think, "who cares?" but as a motorcyclist, you must remain acutely aware of the dangers you face on the road and realize that any imprecision could be your last. Sadly, it happens every day that good riders, following good procedures and riding safely are killed by inattentive drivers, bad conditions, bad judgment, and sometimes just plain bad luck.

The premise of a good self-assessment strategy is that good riders simply do not make mistakes and therefore no mistake can be treated with indifference. Riders must aspire to a high level of precision, placing the wheels exactly where they want them at all times, remaining smooth on the controls, maintaining appropriate speeds and following distances regardless of the factors faced by the rider.

Good Judgment Comes From Experience and a Lot of That Comes From Bad Judgment. -Will Rogers

Some people say we learn from our mistakes. Well of course, we learn from our mistakes. We learn from everything. What is important isn't that we learn, what's important is *what* we learn. Throughout this book, one consistent theme is that a rider must learn from little mistakes because no one will live long enough to make all the big ones. What follows in this section is a list of common mistakes that require immediate analysis to uncover the underlying faults in the rider's present condition so that they are not repeated. After that, the last section discusses how riders can analyze their mistakes, look at the factors that cause them, and recognize key factors which indicate an increased risk of making a similar mistake in the near future.

NINE COMMON MISTAKES REQUIRING EVALUATION

This is not a comprehensive list of mistakes. As riders gain experience, they discover countless situations that they could have handled better, but keeping an open mind to these encounters, they find opportunities for critical evaluation.

MISTAKE ONE- Traveling too close to other traffic

Tailgating increases a rider's risk by decreasing the safety margin between the motorcycle and the vehicle in front. Sometimes this is a useful strategy to improve the flow of traffic, with the rider preferring to create an elastic flow, rather than applying the brakes at every hint of the slightest slow down ahead, but most of the time, it makes absolutely no sense. Even for aggressive drivers who use their large SUV or car to intimidate other vehicles on the road, riders should be realistic: cars aren't intimidated by tailgating motorcyclists. If anything, it is likely to confuse them, possibly causing the driver to slow down farther or hit the brakes.

When riders decide to engage in close travel, they open themselves up to the unpredictability of other vehicles and this should only be done with a clear view of the road ahead and a conscious expectation that the driver ahead may do something surprising such as making a sudden turn or an abrupt stop for seemingly no reason.

So while it may be acceptable to occasionally creep closer to another vehicle ahead and lose a bit of the space cushion, it must be remembered that it is crucial to cover the brakes when losing space cushion and even this must become a safety consideration when the rider continually encroaches on another car's bumper. Remember, there is no time saved by tailgating. It has no effect on your speed except perhaps to cause the driver in front to slow down even more.

Common causes of tailgating include fatigue, impatience, aggression, and inattention.

MISTAKE TWO- Riding in a pack alongside other vehicles

A frequent mantra in motorcycling is to ride your own ride. When riders start to latch onto other traffic, they face a number of risks by relying on the other vehicles. Riders often inadvertently move along with a pack of traffic because it lightens the mental workload by allowing them to rely on the eyes and judgment of the vehicles around them. But can this judgment really be trusted? What's more, can riders really trust other drivers to look out for them? Will other motorists consider the rider before trying to save their own car or bike should the situation demand such a decision be made?

There are simply too many cases of drivers creeping into a motorcyclist's lane or, even worse, abruptly charging in when their needs suddenly dictate a change. Are you as a rider willing to let others dictate where you wind up? Likely, whatever the other traffic sees ahead will soon be affecting you as well and they then make your situation worse by forcing you to deal, not just with the matter ahead, but also take evasive action due to their decisions.

While riders cannot avoid traffic, they can ensure that any issues and dangers are spotted far up the road, that they are acting on the situation, rather than reacting to it. To do this, riders must maintain their own independence of thought and make their own decisions. While riders may be forced to travel along with a pack of traffic, it is crucial for a rider to avoid becoming a part of it.

Common causes of joining a pack include fatigue, laziness, or mental overload.

MISTAKE THREE- Crossing the lines in the road

In certain times and certain places, riders may cross the line in a safe manner, consciously choosing to take a turn a little faster than usual, planning ahead, figuring that they can cross the line safely at a particular moment and be willing to do this deliberately if the bike won't hold the tighter line. While the semi-planned transgression can be a reasonable way of learning a bike's limits, it nevertheless is a mistake to be analyzed. Consider why the

bike wouldn't lean farther and why you didn't initiate the turn sooner. There will always be room for improvement when learning to corner on a motorcycle.

More disturbing, however, are the times the rider crosses a line in the road due to distraction. Perhaps the rider was caught looking at people, or a billboard, and the next thing they knew, they were straddling the centerline. While it may be harmless one particular time, the diligent rider engaged in self-assessment will be well advised to consider the possibly lethal effects of this slight mistake under the wrong circumstances.

Common causes of crossing the lines include fatigue, poor technique, insufficient grip, obstacle fixation, excessive speed.

MISTAKE FOUR- Missing traffic control signs/signals

Not just stop signs, but any signal missed on the road could place a rider in jeopardy. Lane merges, upcoming turns, and changes in speed limits all reflect information that a rider should be aware of. Failure to notice a sign in a timely

manner indicates a lack of awareness on the part of the rider. Even rolling through stop signs is a mistake indicating that the rider likely did not allow adequate opportunity to look in all directions with both eyes.

Common causes of missing or failing to heed traffic control signs/signals include not be looking far enough down the road, distraction, fatigue, excessive speed for the conditions.

MISTAKE FIVE- Failing to see vehicles or road hazards far enough up the road

Under normal circumstances, the rider should be looking well ahead in the direction of travel. When a rider fails to notice pot holes or tires in the road, or any other hazard with adequate time to react well in advance, it opens the rider up to the possibility that some truly critical hazard will go unnoticed.

When riders fail to notice other vehicles surrounding them, they open the possibility that the unnoticed vehicle may do something unpredicted, which places the rider in peril.

Common causes of failing to identify a vehicle or hazard up the road include not looking far enough down the road, distraction, inadequate visual scan technique, fatigue, distraction or zoning out, following too closely, and excessive speed for the road.

MISTAKE SIX- Losing balance while slowing down or stopping

For an experienced rider, maintaining control of a motorcycle during low speed maneuvers should not be difficult. Wobbling at low speed, inadvertently abrupt stops, or placing feet down to retain balance are immediate indications that the rider is not in their usual good form.

Common causes of failing to maintain balance when slowing or stopping may include a problem with tires or suspension, fatigue, distraction, or a medical problem or condition such as hypothermia, hyperthermia, or dehydration.

MISTAKE SEVEN- Inadvertent changes in speed

Occasional slips on the throttle may occur from time to time, but when the rider is repeatedly rolling on and off the throttle, there is likely a problem that needs to be addressed. While throttle locks are handy tools for long distance riding, they are meant to reduce wrist soreness; they are not intended to cover up signs of fatigue or inattention. If you are using a throttle lock or cruise control to avoid having to watch your speed, you probably aren't in the right frame of mind to be on a motorcycle. Perhaps some rest or a cup of coffee might do some good instead.

Common causes of failing to maintain a steady speed include fatigue and distraction.

MISTAKE EIGHT- Failing to check all directions before proceeding to turn or enter an intersection

Sometimes a rider will get lazy and assume that there is no traffic coming from a particular direction. This is most likely to occur on familiar streets. However, familiarity can be the motorcyclist's enemy.

Common causes of failing to check all directions before proceeding include distraction, laziness, or being in a hurry.

MISTAKE NINE- Any situation that forces you to take evasive action in a short matter of time

If a rider is suddenly surprised by an animal, vehicle, or other occurrence, it is likely that they weren't paying enough attention, or weren't thinking thoroughly about possible outcomes given the conditions they were faced with. Perhaps insufficient attention was paid to environmental risks.

Common causes of rapid evasive actions include inattention, distraction, "zoning out", laziness, or excessive speed.

ANALYZING YOUR MISTAKES

When analyzing a mistake, there are typically multiple lessons to be gleaned from the experience. Rider errors are typically not of a single cause, but are made due to a variety of factors that come together. The following is a list of factors that should be considered when assessing a mistake that is made while riding. The following are some common challenges which motorcyclists must face. They must either be accommodated, overcome, or the bike should remain on its side stand.

Mental State- Are you ready to quickly assess the situations that arise? Are you rushed? Distracted? Over-excited? Irritated? Tired? Exhausted?

Physical State- How ready is your body for the ride? Sleepy? Over-caffeinated? Sore? Uncomfortable? Things like being wet, tired, or sore can impact your willingness to contribute 100% attention to the ride. It increases the risk of laziness and prevents you

from being as sharp as you could be.

Road Conditions- Not just the road conditions you have seen, but those that you expect to see, or anticipate may be out there. Bad Weather? Lots of gravel? Darkness? Sun in your eyes? Narrow road? Curvy road?

Traffic Conditions- Heavy Traffic? Pedestrians? Complex riding scenarios involving multiple risks? Complex scenarios require additional caution, not because of what the rider expects might happen, but because of what the rider might never expect to happen. As more people are packed into the rider's surroundings, the more likely the rider will be surprised by someone's actions and the more important it becomes to prepare for the possible unpredictability of each person's actions.

Experience- How did your previous experience prepare you for this moment? Familiar streets? Track-like conditions? Technical or challenging road? Rush hour? Even an experienced long-distance rider may give pause before tackling downtown Chicago in rush hour. Similarly, an experienced city rider may give pause before tackling a technically-demanding mountain road. What's important isn't just your overall experience, but also your level of experience with events which are similar to those you are likely to face.

EXAMPLES

When analyzed carefully, what appears to be the simplest of mistakes often has multiple causes. For example, being distracted by a billboard which causes the rider to weave closely to the centerline might seem to be a simple distraction, but the factors go deeper than that. Perhaps traffic conditions were light, lulling the rider into a false sense of safety. Or, perhaps, the rider has other things on the mind that are making it difficult to focus 100% on the ride. Perhaps the rider is tired. To be certain, this is a small mistake that occurs frequently, but by refusing to let even minor transgressions escape scrutiny, riders can push themselves to be better and safer.

Mistakes are seldom of a single cause. Riders should always seek to discover the secondary and tertiary causes of mistakes they make. Even if a cause seems insignificant, every tiny mistake offers the rider an opportunity to discover environmental and situational hazards that they may not have fully appreciated just moments before. Using this self-assessment strategy, the more critical the rider becomes of tiny mistakes, the more adept the rider will become at identifying hazards that may be a far greater factor sometime shortly down the road.

THE BASIC MATH TEST

Regardless of your particular mathematical abilities, the Basic Math Test is an exceptional test for fatigue. What is important is not the difficulty of the problems, but rather your ability to solve them.

Everyone can do some type of math problem in their head. Whether it is addition, subtraction, multiplication, or division, single digits, double, or more is unimportant. You can just choose random numbers, although I usually prefer to calculate things such as gas mileage or the number of minutes until the next stop, as it seems to be of more practical value.

The concept behind the Basic Math Test is that you create math problems that should be easily solvable in your head and informally assess your ability to solve them. As you get more fatigued, you will notice a dramatic decline in your ability to solve these types of problems. With practice, this can become a good indicator of when you need to stop and take a rest.

CARRYING A PILLION

8

Pillion– n. 1. A second saddle for an additional rider on a motorcycle; 2. The person riding on the pillion seat.

the pillion is an active part of the ride. It is the pillion's job to help the rider make the ride as smooth as possible.

Choosing to take a pillion is a personal decision that is fraught with many risks and rewards. It is primarily the rider's responsibility to ensure the pillion's safety and enjoyment of the ride. Hopefully the following tips will help.

There are no passengers on motorcycles- passengers are passive. Even a light pillion on a motorcycle can add one-third or more weight to the bike, and this additional weight presents a number of challenges. With the weight of a pillion, the motorcycle will not stop as quickly, accelerate as briskly, or turn as crisply. In addition, the extra weight on the back can throw off the bike's center of balance, further reducing the bike's ability to turn in the corners. Unlike a passenger in a car,

GEARING UP YOUR PILLION

What goes for the rider ought to go double for the pillion with regard to safety. I personally feel that pillions should generally be offered more protection than the rider wears. After all, the rider knows better than the pillion what they are getting into, but for many pillions, it is a new or rare experience. By shopping off-season and looking for deals, it is possible for motorcyclists to fully outfit their

With the weight of a pillion, the motorcycle will not stop as quickly, accelerate as briskly, or turn as crisply

pillion without breaking the bank. If you don't have a regular pillion, you can simply buy gear to fit the size of the pillion you are ideally looking for.

A spare set of gloves is easy enough to keep tucked under the seat and is nice for the rider to have around from time to time anyway. In addition to being good to offer a pillion, they will be appreciated by the rider when the first pair gets sweaty, wet, or otherwise uncomfortable.

A spare riding jacket can also be had cheaply enough on closeout. Unfortunately, pants sizing is probably too variable to really be a practical for an unplanned pillion. However, jeans or other long pants are a little bit better than nothing.

A lot of riders keep only a single helmet, which they will chivalrously offer to their new pillion before a ride. This may be okay if the rider is willing to ride without a helmet and the motorcycle has a backrest, but on a sportbike, even the most well-intentioned pillion will occasionally be banging the helmet into the rider's head. Ouch! Most bikes have a place to securely lock a spare helmet. Besides, if you're single, the spare helmet is a great advertisement.

MOUNTING THE BIKE

Before a pillion gets on the bike, it is important for the rider to be set up and ready. The rider should brace the bike with feet spread out at a slightly exaggerated distance to help with the expected weight-shift when the pillion gets on. From this position, the rider's thighs will catch the bike if it starts to tilt. Of course, the motor will already be running at this time because it needs to be warmed up before taking off, and the bike will be in neutral with the front brake on to keep the bike from rolling, even slightly, as the pillion is getting on.

Pillions should mount the bike with their weight over the centerline of the tires. In other words, they should lean over the bike as they are getting on. They should not place their foot on the peg and try to pull themselves up onto the bike. Even for the lightest of pillions and the heaviest of bikes, this can skew the center of balance and cause the bike to fall down on themselves and the rider.

For standard bikes without back rests or tall sissy bars, the best way for a taller pillion to mount the bike is from behind. This way, no matter how they mount the bike, their weight will be completely along the centerline. In the city, the rider can often back the bike up to a curb to allow easier mounting, especially for shorter pillions or taller bikes. In parking lots, a concrete tire stop may also work well to give the pillion a little help getting up onto the rearsets of taller bikes.

PILLIONS SHOULD KEEP THEIR FEET ON THE PEGS

The pillion's feet should remain on the pegs. On most bikes, pillions trying to put their feet down will risk getting burned on the hot exhaust pipes. In addition, most pavement is actually surprisingly slippery, especially around intersections. Riders therefore may need to move their feet forward and backward in order to find adequate footing. The last thing the rider wants is to step on someone else's toes while trying to keep the bike from falling.

THE PILLION SHOULD WAIT UNTIL THE BIKE IS STABLE BEFORE REPOSITIONING

A bike is least stable when it is moving slowly. When stopped, the rider's feet provide additional stability and when underway the centrifugal force keeps the bike easily upright. Therefore, pillions should remain the most still while the bike is coming to a stop or moving at an unusually slow speed. Slight readjustments for comfort are best performed either while underway, or when the rider's feet are down during a complete stop.

PILLIONS SHOULD MAINTAIN PROPER POSITIONING DURING TURNS

As a bike starts to lean into a turn, sensing that they are about to fall, the unpracticed pillion is likely to try and lean to the outside, against the turn. Or, the overly-enthusiastic pillion might try to lean into the turn, exaggerating the motions of the rider. Either of these is likely to do more harm than good, especially with an inexperienced pillion. Some people advise the pillion to sit "like a sack of potatoes" and not move at all. This also is not an optimal strategy.

Instead of fighting the motion of the motorcycle, exaggerating it, or remaining motionless, the easiest way for the pillion to complement the motions of the motorcycle during a turn is to look over the rider's shoulder in the direction of the turn. For example, when turning to the right, the pillion should look over the rider's right shoulder and during left turns, the left shoulder. This ensures that the pillion won't resist the motions of the

the easiest way for the pillion to compliment the motions of the motorcycle during a turn is to look over the rider's shoulder in the direction of the turn

bike while also providing just enough of a lean to help a little.

PILLIONS SHOULD HOLD ONTO THE RIDER WHILE ACCELERATING

Even when the acceleration begins slowly and leisurely, the possibility exists that the rider may have to suddenly twist the throttle hard due to changing situations. Therefore, when accelerating, the pillion should always lean slightly forward and hold onto the rider's waist, especially if the bike is not equipped with a sissy bar or backrest. Pillions may also squeeze their knees against the rider's waist to help remain in position. The pillion should know to always expect the possibility of sudden acceleration.

THE PILLION SHOULD AVOID BUMPING HEADS WITH THE RIDER

When braking, the pillion must be careful not to bump helmets with the rider. It's annoying for the rider and will possibly damage the helmets. Pillions should maintain control of their body and keep it properly positioned at all times.

PILLIONS SHOULD SUPPORT THEIR OWN WEIGHT WHEN BRAKING

Especially on standard/sportbikes, a lot of pressure is placed on the rider's wrists during braking. If the pillion is pressing up against the rider, this effectively doubles the load on the rider's wrists and will very quickly cause soreness and fatigue. Therefore, the pillion should place his/her hands on the gas tank when coming to a stop and use their arms to support their own weight. This will reduce pressure on the rider's wrists and back and make longer or more traffic-congested rides go a lot smoother.

THE RIDER AND PILLION SHOULD SET UP SIGNALS

It is difficult to communicate on the bike. So before taking off, it is wise to set up a series of basic hand signals. Some of the more common things to communicate include:

Bathroom/water/stretch break
Stop Immediately
Slow Down
I want to get off

The signals should be clear enough that they won't be confused with pointing things out.

If a rider expects to ride more than a brief distance with a pillion, it is best that they work out these signals ahead of time or else they will most assuredly be figuring them out along the way.

WEIGHT AND BALANCE

Sportbikes are specifically designed for approximately a 52/48 weight distribution front to rear. Any substantial deviation from this, regardless of the type of bike, will reduce the vehicle's handling ability. Bearing in mind that a light bike may weigh less than 400 pounds, you can imagine the effect of a 150 pound pillion sitting almost over the rear wheel. The balance that the manufacturer so carefully designed into the bike is thrown out the window. While you can (and should) raise the shock and add a couple psi to the tires, the bike still isn't going to handle the same.

From a handling standpoint, the best place to store things is under the seat as it tends to have the least effect on center of gravity. For similar reasons, saddle bags are to be preferred over top cases (unless narrow streets or lane splitting is a concern). The more the center of gravity is raised and moved rearward, the lighter your front tire will become, which reduces your handling in the turns. As you add more weight, the tires squish down a little more, the shocks compress under the additonal weight, your acceleration and braking are diminished as well.

SELECTING GEAR 9

There's one seldom-mentioned piece of equipment to consider carrying with you: cash. Cell phones don't work everywhere, credit cards don't work everywhere, but money does work everywhere. It's wise to keep a small stash securely tucked underneath the seat of your motorcycle, just for emergencies. Ideally, maintain an assortment of bills because there's no guarantee that you'll be able to break a hundred when you need to.

There is a greater variety of riding gear available today than ever before; there is a helmet for every head shape, a jacket for every body, and a pair of boots that fits for the racer who never walks beyond the paddock as well as the touring rider who hikes for hours. If you can't find something that works for you, there are even companies that make custom gear. There are styles for every rider, from radical race-inspired designs, to simple black leather and everything in between. Innovative features also abound; some gear is packed with features you never even knew you needed, but will soon learn you can't live with out.

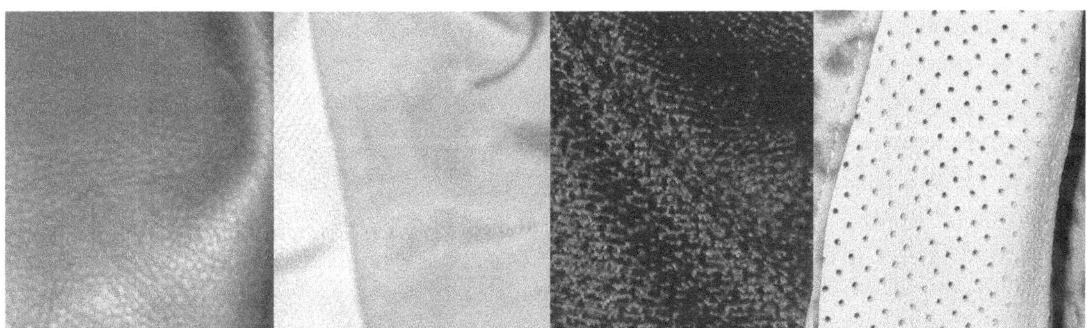

Leather, Nylon, Nylon mesh, and Perforated Leather. All offer a unique combination of protection and comfort at varying price points and for varying climates.

LEATHER, TEXTILES, AND MESH

Leather is the most common material used in motorcycle gear construction. It's been around forever and it works. Some leather is perforated to allow airflow in warmer climates. Leather is typically classified by the millimeter, with thicker, stiffer, more protective cowhide leather being around 1.4 to 1.5mm and slightly thinner leather being used where flexibility is more crucial. Not all leather, however, is the same. Kangaroo leather, for example, offers significantly better abrasion resistance and is also significantly thinner than cowhide. It is most frequently seen on the palms of gloves where tactile feel is important to the rider.

There are many types of textiles used in motorcycling. For protection, the most common are ballistic nylon and aramid fibers (such as the DuPont's name brand Kevlar®). Ballistic nylon, often sold under the tradename of Cordura®, is frequently used in touring-oriented gear due to its water-resistance and ease of fabrication. Though less abrasion-resistant than leather, it is substantially lighter and ease of fabrication allows for many features to be sewn into the garment.

While nobody disputes the fact that leather and nylon are more protective than skin, hotter weather often finds riders opting for comfort over protection- mesh gear is typically made of loosely-woven nylon and is generally lighter in weight. It seldom provides the same degree of protection as other gear. However, as a cooler and safer alternative to jeans or tee-shirts, it is a wise and comfortable investment.

Aramid thread, such as that sold under the brand name of Kevlar®, has been around for awhile in motorcycling, providing stitching on leather and other garments due to its high tensile strength. It is normally yellow in color, although it can be dyed. Aramids offer many of the advantages of ballistic nylon with greater abrasion resistance than even leather. Presently, it is still fairly expensive and at the time of this writing, there is no standard thickness or weave for motorcycling gear, so all such gear must be carefully evaluated by the purchaser for suitability for motorcycling.

PROTECTIVE ARMOR

Armor provides protection from three types of injuries: abrasion, impact, and puncture. Abrasion injuries occur when a rider slides across the pavement. The sliding motion tends to wear down the protective layer. Impact injuries occur when a rider collides with a hard object. Puncture injuries are somewhat rare, but occur when armor is impaled by a sharp object.

Armor can be hard or soft. Hard armor, typically plastic, provides abrasion and puncture resistance. It is found as a knuckle guard on some gloves, occasionally on the outside of other garments, and is worn frequently while off-roading. One weakness of hard armor, however, is often its method of attachment. A prospective buyer should look carefully at the seams, noting how the hard armor is attached. Since hard armor does not flex like the leather it is typically attached to, it may be prone to tear off in an accident. Ask yourself if it is likely to tear off and, if it did, what kind of protection you would be left with.

Soft armor is typically some sort of foam. Sometimes buyers will encounter cheap foam that may only be an eighth of an inch thick and feels like a wet sponge. Generally, this is used in fashion jackets to give the appearance of protection and bulk, but it's rather worthless in an impact. What riders want is stiff foam that is hard to compress. Remember, the purpose of this foam is not to let the rider down soft like a baby into a crib, but to absorb just enough impact to keep the rider from shattering bones when slammed against the pavement.

Armor may be certified. The European Union has a certification for soft and hard protective armor. Armor meeting these standards will have an ECE approval stamped into them somewhere. At this time, there is no comparable U.S. standard for what constitutes armor.

CARBON FIBER ARMOR

Some companies offer hard armor piece made of "carbon fiber". This is often just for fashion and is seldom seen on high end gear except for expensive helmets where the weight savings is significant. Cheaper ABS plastic is softer and flexes more, often providing more consistent protection when attached to leather riding gear.

SEAMS

Looking at the seams on a motorcycle garment can tell you a lot about the quality of its construction. Not just a matter of how pretty they look,

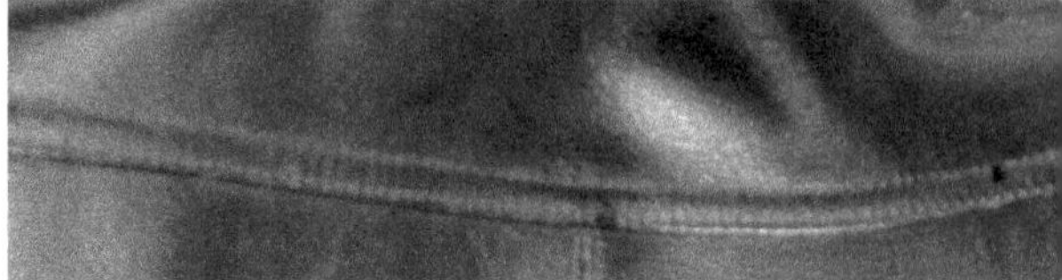

A double-stitched seam.

different seams are particularly well-suited for different portions of a garment.

Double-stitched seams provide the most tear-strength, making them ideal for the seams requiring the most strength. However, double-stitched seams tend to be thick and if they are tight against the rider's body, may begin to rub.

Outside seams are generally pretty ugly to look at, but they serve a great purpose. By keeping the seam on the outside, the inside is smoother and more comfortable for the rider. This is of particular importance on items such as gloves which are intended to fit very tightly against the rider's body.

Another consideration when looking at seams is to remember their tendency to fall apart once they have begun to unravel. For this reason, many manufacturers prefer shorter curved or zig-zagged seams rather than long straight lines. In an accident where the force on the seam is from one direction, the unraveling of the seam will tend to stop when it reaches the curve or zig-zag.

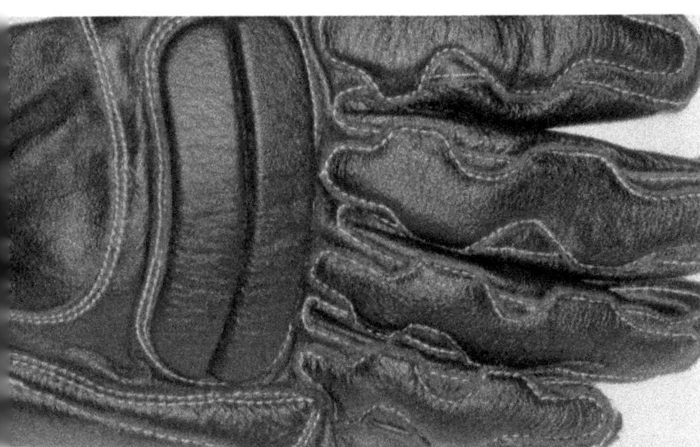

Notice that there is not a single straight seam anywhere on this glove. Curved seams are less likely to shred apart during a slide across the pavement.

JACKETS

Generally, it is wise to select riding gear from a respectable manufacturer of riding apparel. The "fashion" jackets may look comparable from a distance, but the protective features you need may not be there under close inspection. In fact, even some manufacturers of riding gear sometimes miss the mark and release lesser quality jackets with regard to the qualities presented above.

Some features to consider which are unique to riding jackets include:

Air Control– Will the jacket be windproof in colder weather? Will it be cool enough when it gets hot? Many jackets provide vents which zip open to provide airflow and can be closed when the temperatures get cooler. Perforated leather is great when the temperatures are higher, but can't be closed when it starts to rain or when the temperature drops.

Liners– Some gear comes with zip-in liners. These may provide insulation from the cold, water-resistance, wind resistance, or some combination of the three. Keeping the wind off your body is an amazingly effective way to keep warm when the temperature drops. Just preventing the breeze from hitting your body at 30 to 70mph can be the difference between cold shivers and complete comfort when temperatures are cooler.

Adjustability– In order for a jacket to do its job, it needs to fit snugly so it's not sliding around during a crash. Adjustable buckles or straps can give a piece of gear an almost-custom feel as well as provide for the gain or loss of a couple of pounds.

Back flap– A more aggressive sport riding position, with the rider leaning

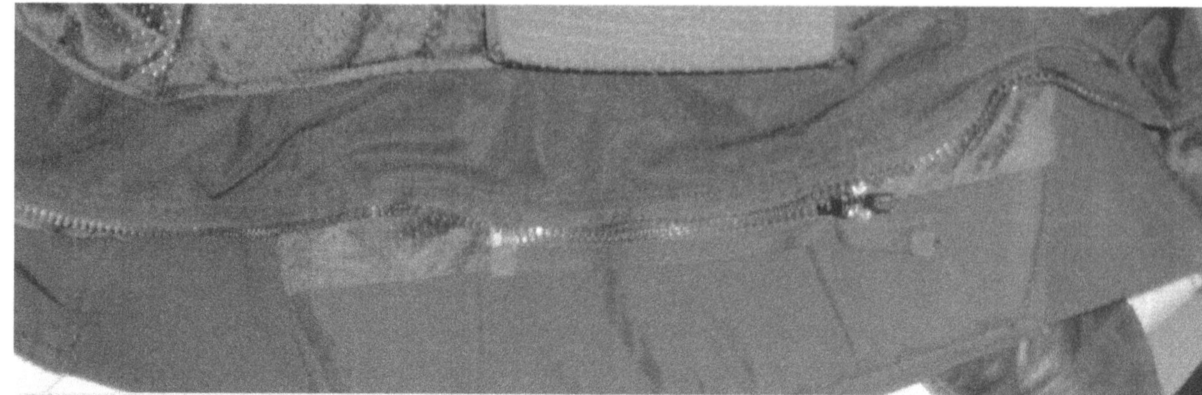

This jacket has both a shorter 8" zipper in the middle as well as a full-circumference zipper. Having both options sewn into a jacket doubles the chances of finding a pair of pants to zip into them. In addition to different lengths, note as well that some zippers go right to left, while others go left to right.

forward, will tend to expose the lower back. Sport jackets are often cut longer in the back to keep the rider covered, adding to comfort on longer rides.

Pants Zippers– Many sport riding jackets offer a zipper along the bottom of the jacket. These are meant to zip into riding pants. Note that not all zipper configurations are compatible. While some manufacturers may work together, others do not. You will also find that zippers come in different lengths. There are full-circumference zippers that go all the way around your body, making the riding pants and jacket effectively into a single-piece which holds everything together, keeping the jacket from riding up, or pants from sliding down, during a slide. Less effective, but still far better than nothing is the 6 to 8" zipper in the back of the garment that allows the jacket and pants to zip together in a more convenient, though somewhat less secure, manner.

PANTS

A variety of options exist for riders looking to protect their lower body from injury during a crash. Padded undergarments provide padding in strategic locations such as the knees and hips. This may offer some impact protection, but does little to provide the abrasion resistance that a rider needs for even low-speed slides. In addition, undergarments may be bulky, sweaty, and difficult to take off when away from home.

For convenience, some riders opt for a pair of Kevlar® or aramid jeans, which make use of highly abrasion-resistant fabrics in strategic locations such as the knees and hips. This is a viable option for those looking to provide a degree of protection without having to carry around a load of riding gear when reaching the destination. Still, the lack of armor for puncture and impact protection can leave the rider dangerously exposed during a crash. Also, denim itself provides little protection, as evidence by any child who grew up playing football in the streets. Certainly for as little protection as denim offers from scraped knees and bicycle mishaps, it can hardly be expected to hold up well to the significantly greater forces involved in motorcycling.

A better option for those looking to get on and off a motorcycle with normal street clothes would be a pair of overpants. These garments are designed to go on and off easily, often with a full-length zipper along the sides. While slightly bulky, they can provide a more abrasion resistant fabric than jeans, a greater amount of padding than undergarments, and allow the rider the option of taking them off after reaching the destination. Storage for overpants can be as easy as placing them in a motorcycle top case, but for most bikes, a simple bicycle lock with a plastic-coated wire can be run through the arms or legs of the gear and around the bike frame to create some security while away from the bike.

Many riders like to wear pants when they ride. Some choose to place their faith in blue jeans to protect them in a crash, but from experience as an 8 year old boy playing football in the streets of Chicago, I never had a pair that didn't shred to ribbons with the slightest scrape against the concrete. Given this, I have little faith that blue jeans will hold up any better at the higher speeds often associated with motorcycling.

The safest option for riding pants is properly-fitting leather pants. Without the generous sizes required for overpants, regular riding pants are less prone to slide around during a crash– this helps to ensure the armor is exactly where it should be when body parts strike the ground. The tighter fit will also reduce the severity of "rug burn" in the event of a higher-energy crash. The trade-off, of course, is less comfort while off the bike and the inability to remove the gear in public.

BOOTS

The needs of a rider are very unique when it comes to footwear. Most street boots offer a compromise between the characteristics of an extreme racing boot and the all-day comfort of ordinary shoes. First we will look into some of the considerations that go into a quality racing boot. From there, readers can determine what safety protections are desirable for the kind of riding they do.

The perfect riding boot should be stiff enough to keep the ankle joint from bending in a crash; protect the front of the shin from anything that may be standing up in the road; protect the ball of the ankle should the rider fall to the side; provide a stiff sole to keep the foot from being crushed under the bike; provide a toe slider to prevent the toe getting caught against the pavement at high lean angles; provide adequate traction when the rider's feet touch down on a slippery road; be thin and narrow enough for the rider's feet to comfortably fit between the peg and the controls.

Some things to avoid when looking for a riding boot include long shoe laces that can get caught in the bike chain; a loose fit (a normal hiking boot can easily fly off your foot during a high-energy crash); too flexible which provides little protection from extension/reflection-type injuries; too thick in the toe to easily slide between the peg and the shifter.

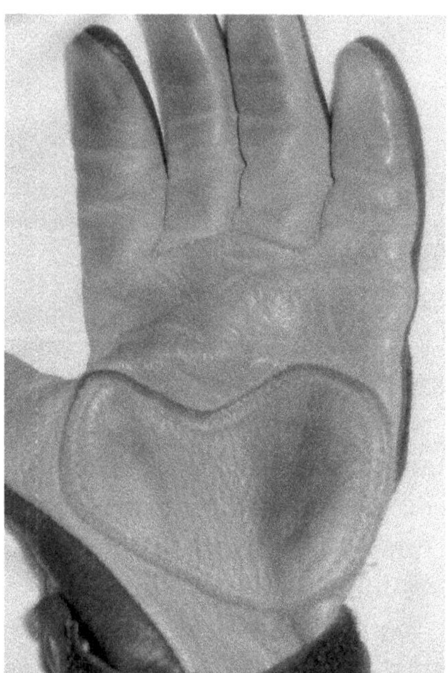

GLOVES

Gloves provide a dry predictable surface with which to contact the controls of the bike. Gloves can also provide warmth in cold weather, keep hands cool in hot weather, and dry in wet weather. They can even help prevent a broken wrist.

When trying on gloves, check for seams which rub against skin, this can create a rash or soreness during an extended ride. Poorly made gloves will rub against the hand or fingers, causing irritation. To further customize the fit of a glove, it is possible to buy glove liners to make a slightly loose glove fit a little more snugly.

In addition to the abrasion resistance provided by leather, gloves may also have a low-friction surface on the palm to prevent the rider from reaching out and planting their hands during a fall, which is an instinctive reaction, but a dangerous one that can easily result in a broken wrist.

Finally, many gloves have protective bits of hard plastic as a knuckle guard. While these provide a lot of puncture protection, they often will not flex much, which may cause them to tear away from the glove in an accident. These impact zones, such as the knuckles and bottom of the palm certainly deserve additional protection, but due to the type of injuries that are common to the hands, extra leather or padding may actually be a better option than hard plastic.

HELMETS

No article of riding gear is as likely to save a rider's life as a helmet. The process of informed helmet selection involves understanding a variety of different technical standards and how they relate to the risks and hazards that are likely to be encountered. There is a hodge-podge of different standards, requirements, rules and regulations regarding helmets. All readers are encouraged to learn more about these varying standards and come to their own decision as to what is best. It is wise for riders to seek out the safest, not necessarily the most legal, riding gear for the type of riding they will do.

Helmets serve many functions on a daily basis. They protect from weather such as rain and wind, and also prevent debris such as small rocks or bugs from striking the rider's face. However, the primary purpose of a helmet is to protect against three main types of injury– penetration (such as falling on a sharp pointy object that could enter the skull); abrasion (sliding down the road); and, most importantly, deceleration (the rider's head coming to a rapid stop against a solid object such as another vehicle or the ground). To protect from these risks, a helmet consists of two protective components: the outer shell and the inner shell.

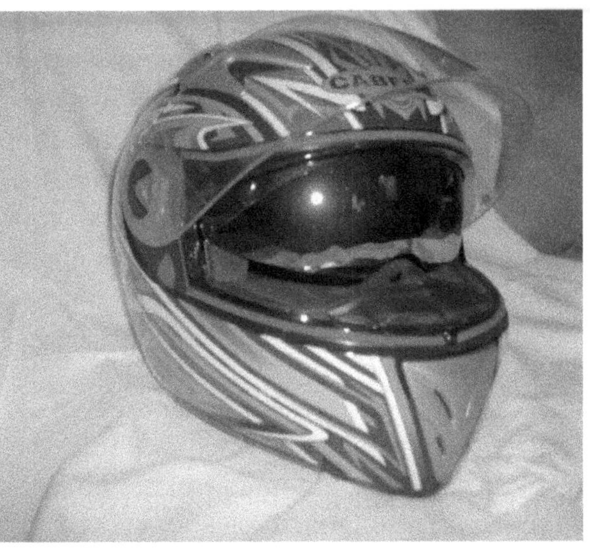

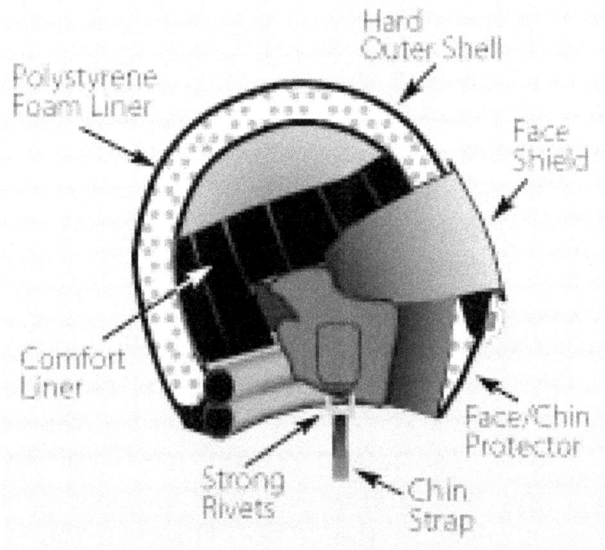

The Inner Shell

The inner shell consists of a foam material, often polystyrene which is intended to compress during a crash in order to absorb the impact. Once compressed, the inner liner does not expand back to its original shape– this is one of many reasons that helmets should be considered one-time-use items.

Attached to this shell, there is another softer liner or "comfort foam" which compresses and decompresses repeatedly and is intended to help the helmet fit more comfortably with the exact contours of an oddly-shaped head. Often this comfort pad is removable and washable. When doing so, it is a good idea to inspect the inner shell and check for any indication of damage or wear to the inner shell. While this inspection is not adequate to ensure that the helmet is safe, it can be used to reject a damaged helmet. Due to the importance of the inner shell and its inability to endure multiple impacts, any significant shock to the helmet should be considered cause to replace it.

The Outer Shell

Outer shells typically consist of a relatively firm material which is abrasion-resistant. The most common materials are either a thermoformed plastic or else a composite material. At this time, there is no evidence that one of these materials is better than the other. Thermoformed plastic such as ABS is generally the cheapest, softest, and most flexible option. The soft plastic shells are less gouge-resistant and many riders find the thermoformed plastics to feel "cheap". Indeed, the lightness and texture may indeed make them feel like a child's toy. But is it such a bad option?

When a helmet strikes an object, the goal is to spread the force of impact onto as large an area of the inner shell as possible, thereby reducing the pressure on the inner shell and absorbing more of the impact before it reaches the rider's skull. The flexibility of thermoplastics often allows the inner liner to absorb impacts more evenly over a wider area. In addition, the reduced weight helps to reduce strain on the rider's neck on longer duration rides and may reduce the risk or severity of whiplash.

The other option, composite shells, tend to be stiffer and heavier. The most expensive helmets at this time use carbon fiber, which is just about as light as the thermoplastics, although significantly stiffer and harder. The hardness of composites helps to prevent nicks and gouges, which reduce the appearance over time. Most riders find that the composite helmets feel stiffer, more substantial, and of better quality. However, there is no evidence that they provide any greater safety.

Composite shells absorb impact somewhat differently than thermoplastics. Whereas thermoplastics tend to bend and flex during impact to spread the forces along a greater area of the inner shell, composites tend to delaminate. The delamination of the composite helmet during impact absorbs energy that would otherwise be transferred to the inner shell and into the rider's head. After an impact such as a crash or even just falling off the seat or handlebar of a bike, delamination of the outer shell can occur, reducing the ability of the helmet to absorb impacts in the future. It is important to realize that delamination is not always visible through the paint or graphics on a helmet. Riding around with a compressed or cracked inner liner or a delaminated or distressed outer liner places the rider at greater risk of severe head injury. Helmets must always be maintained in top condition to work their best.

Helmet Standards

When selecting a helmet, there are three different stamps of approval- DOT, SNELL 2010, and ECE 22-05. The DOT standard is the legally-required standard in the United States. Simply put, if it doesn't meet the DOT specification, it can't be sold as a protective helmet in the USA. However, the DOT standard is self-applied and does not require actual testing, only "certification" by the manufacturer that it meets the standard. To ensure you are wearing a DOT helmet, the rider can look for the following stamp:

DOT

The Economic Community of Europe has another standard called ECE 22-05. The ECE standard is generally recognized as more stringent, though the two standards are not mutually exclusive.

CE

In general, both the DOT and ECE standards are focused on accidents involving low speed helmet strikes because, although motorcycles can travel quickly, head impacts usually occur against the ground at a relatively low downward speed.

There is also a common non-governmental standard known as SNELL 2010. The Snell Memorial Foundation runs an independent testing lab and provides actual physical tests, to their own standards, for helmets. In practice, it appears that many Snell-rated helmets perform marginally worse on the low-energy tests required by the ECE and DOT, subjecting the head to slightly higher impact forces, while providing greater protection in more unusal higher-energy crashes.

Ultimately, riders must make their own decision as to what helmet and standards are important to them. It may be useful to note that most riders in Moto-GP, the motorcycle equivalent of Formula 1 auto racing, typically use helmets rated to the ECE 22-05 standard. It may also be useful to note that there is no specific number of G-forces that will specifically cause head trauma. It is a sliding scale in which more G-force is worse and less is always better.

Another consideration for riders is the weight of a helmet. While not directly considered in the DOT requirements, a lighter helmet generally makes a rider less susceptible to whiplash. The weight of the helmet increases the risk of whiplash if the rider's neck is to be whipped around during a collision. Full face helmets may weigh as little as 2 and a half pounds with 3 and a half pounds being a more typical value.

Some Considerations When Selecting a Helmet:

When checking the fit of a helmet, you want to be sure that it is comfortable on your head.

In general, a lighter well-balanced helmet can reduce fatigue over longer distances.

The cheek pads should press firmly against your cheeks, but not be tight.

With the chin strap secured, grabbing the front chin guard of a full face helmet, it should not be possible to twist or pull the helmet anything more than slightly out of position.

The Proper Fit

Helmets come in a variety of shapes, sizes, and designs. The best shape is the one that fits the rider best. Ratings, certifications, and brand names are worthless if the helmet does not fit properly and provide comfort on every ride and also remain securely on the rider's head throughout a crash. Note that an improperly-fitted helmet will cause pressure points on a rider's head, potentially causing numbness, soreness, and headaches throughout longer rides.

Face Shields

Face shields may come in a variety of shades and colors- in addition to clear and smoked, you may find reflective shields in varying reflective colors and tints. With some helmets, changing a face shield may require a simple tool that you carry with you, while other helmets offer a tool-less system involving some sort of button or lever that can be used to pop out the visor. This may not be a factor for the rider who only switches face shields when one becomes scratched or damaged, however some riders prefer to carry a dark shield for day time riding and a second clear shield for night time riding and will switch frequently. Another option is to purchase a helmet with a built-in sun visor that can be flipped up and down as necessary.

Venting

Most helmets provide some amount of venting. Venting helps keep your head cool and may also help prevent fogging in colder weather. There is no sure way to check for venting without going for an actual ride. However, higher-end helmets tend to have better venting options. Be aware, as well, that vents tend to increase noise within a helmet.

Noise

Motorcycling is noisy regardless of the helmet you select. The best solution to noise is ear plugs. However, a quieter helmet can make any trip more enjoyable. After ear plugs, the next most important factor in helmet noise the way a helmet fits. If it is reasonably snug, a helmet will tend to block noise better. However, helmets are not a suitable replacement for earplugs which provide substantially greater hearing protection.

AFTERWORD

For many riders, the danger and challenge of motorcycling is part of its appeal, but plenty of dangers and challenges exist without the rider compounding them with laziness, inattention, or ignorance. Hopefully this book has reinforced the message that these additional, peripheral, risks deserve no place in motorcycling on top of what's already out there. Indeed, the concept of risk-conscious riding is important, but what's most important is understanding that the dangers do not disappear with knowledge, but rather with implementation.

This book has promoted and encouraged a deeper understanding of risks and dangers, but it cannot diminish them- riders must do that for themselves. So if you feel that this book has brought you valuable insight that will assist you in your implementation of more risk-conscious riding strategies, please pass this book along to a loved one or friend. Spread the word. Encourage discussion.

There is a lot of important and valuable information that, up to now, may have been difficult for riders to obtain through an organized channel. It is my goal to bring this information to the attention of riders. In order to make the widest possible breadth of information available to riders, I will be using the website ArtofStreetRiding.com as a clearinghouse of information for riders. I hope to provide valuable and interesting links and information pertaining to motorcycling, especially related to risk-conscious riding. As always, this information may not represent the majority opinion; it may not be good advice for all riders or at all times. This does not make the information any less valuable for some riders and in some situations. It remains vital for riders to assess the information for themselves and to discuss it with others. It is my belief that these types of discussions, initiated by riders amongst themselves, will ultimately prove to be the most valuable educational tool for risk-conscious riding.

It is my sincerest hope that these lessons, concepts, and ideas presented are as valuable to you as they have been to me. If you feel you have anything to add, or if you have any questions, or even great pictures to share for a second edition, you can contact me through my website at www.ArtofStreetRiding.com. The feedback and assistance I receive may very well encourage me to work on a second edition. However, I want your input and your thoughts. I want to further refine the ideas and concepts I've presented and I am also open to new concepts of risk-conscious riding that you may have developed yourself. In my view, the actual art of street riding, like this book by the same name, is still in its infancy.

Any errors, omissions, or revisions or additions to the book will be made available through ArtofStreetRiding.com. This site will be updated as appropriate with the goal of providing the best possible information to riders in a timely manner. As I have said before, this book remains a work in progress and up to this point has largely been an independent effort. I will attempt to remain available through email and other sources to provide discussion and points for consideration, even when unable to give definitive answers.

Finally, I would like to wish you the best of luck and judgment in your riding adventures, wherever they may take you.

www.ingramcontent.com/pod-product-compliance
Ingram Content Group UK Ltd.
Pitfield, Milton Keynes, MK11 3LW, UK
UKHW051128260726
13967UKWH00010B/2922

9 780578 048307